Managing Leadership

Managing Leadership

❖

Toward a New and Usable Understanding of What Leadership Really is —and How to Manage it

Jim Stroup

iUniverse, Inc.
New York Lincoln Shanghai

Managing Leadership
Toward a New and Usable Understanding of What Leadership Really is—and How to Manage it

iUniverse, Inc.

For information address:
iUniverse, Inc.
2021 Pine Lake Road, Suite 100
Lincoln, NE 68512
www.iuniverse.com

The opinions or assertions contained are those of the writer and are not to be construed as official or reflecting the views of the Marine Corps.

ISBN: 0-595-31551-8

Printed in the United States of America

This book is dedicated to my wife, Emel,
my brother, Michael,
and my friend,
Chuck Martenson

Contents

Part II   *Organizational leadership*

Part III   Conclusion

Acknowledgments

This book is the result of years of learning from others. It is, of course, impossible to thank them all by name. I would like, nevertheless, to express my gratitude for the examples of command, management, and leadership I've learned from colleagues and associates in the U.S. Marine Corps, all of the other military services of the United States, and those of many other countries around the world. There has been plenty of study of examples of individual military leadership, but not enough of military organizations and their members. I am honored to have had the opportunity to serve in and observe such organizations at all levels.

Additionally, I have had the pleasure to work with numerous employees and managers of many international commercial, non-profit, and governmental organizations. I thank them all for their insights and enlightening discussions. These have immeasurably integrated and enriched my appreciation of organizational leadership.

It is necessary, as well, to acknowledge my debt to those who have studied and written in the past about leadership of, or in, organizations, and those who continue to do so. Our insights, opinions, and ideas are never formed in isolation, and the vigor of the dialectic by means of which we discuss them is as at least as important to their vitality as is whatever humble contribution we make ourselves. This field has attracted some of the finest minds working anywhere, and it is with the greatest humility that I offer this modest contribution to the leadership debate.

Finally, I must express my thanks to three individuals without whom this project would never have become a reality. First is Colonel James L. Williams, USMC (Ret.), who is referred to in this book, and with whom I have had the great fortune to serve. His example, teaching, and continued support have been fundamental contributions to the development of the concepts expressed in this book. Next is Turkish business manager and writer Hakan Yaman, whose agile thought process, expansive knowledge and experience, and intense conversation helped crystallize the awareness that this project should be undertaken. I must thank, as well, my wife, Dr. Emel Stroup, for her contributions from the field of clinical psychology and cognitive therapy, for her insightful and valuable editorial and structural reviews, and of course, for her enduring and indispensable faith and support.

Preface

Ralph Waldo Emerson once said that an institution is the lengthened shadow of one man. Those organizations that accept this as referring to the senior executive's personal leadership skills will eventually find themselves to be in deep trouble. Even if the current leader is of exceptional talent and possessed of inspired insight, these abilities will often prove to be essentially time—and situation-based, and will ultimately be overcome by events. Or, his successor will not possess these abilities at the right time, and will destroy an organization that is accustomed to depending on him to provide them.

On the other hand, there is a military dictum that a unit's success or failure is wholly the responsibility of its commander. If that commander chooses to arrogate to himself personally the performance of all the unit's leadership functions, he is as likely, in the end, to prove responsible for its failures, as he is for its achievements. If, however, he is content to use his command authority to marshal and deploy the expression of these leadership functions from all available sources, he greatly increases the likelihood of his organization's, and incidentally his own, success. This does not require superhuman vision or charisma. A manager of quite ordinary technical ability who takes this approach leverages and focuses skills that are widespread throughout the organization. Such a manager demonstrates his superiority through his deference to, and intelligent use of, a powerful organizational asset.

Unfortunately, this approach is not common. Our leaders generally aspire to some form of "great man" status. Yet, this is a concept that we often both celebrate and condemn. For each of those who argue for the great man theory of history or organizational leadership, there are those who counter that our organizations and we are driven by deep and inscrutable trends that surface to give themselves expression through this or that unwitting mouthpiece. Great men are thus more accidents of history than shapers of it. Perhaps it is more accurate to argue, however, that there are indeed great men who can identify and organize these internal forces and turn them to desired purposes, thereby converting us from flotsam carried in their path to channels shaping their direction and power. Among these forces are the natural leadership environment and phenomenon arising from and interacting within human societies. The masters of these forces are those who discern, cultivate, and direct them. The truly great men, then, are not leaders at all. They are those managers, of perhaps quite ordinary skills, who have nevertheless attained this extraordinary insight, and who use it to elevate not themselves, but their organizations.

Why this book was written

For well over thirty years, I have had the good fortune to participate at all levels in organizations of all types throughout the world. During this time, I have also been able to observe and consult with many of these organizations. In the course of this, I have typically detected in them an inconsistent, or even harmful, approach to organizational leadership. Often, this was expressed by a failure to acknowledge, at all, the importance of the influence of leadership in the organization. On other occasions, it was represented by a formulaic and no-exceptions application of a personal general philosophy on the subject to all particular individual and institutional leadership issues. (In truth, that approach, rather than reflecting an actual philosophy of the topic, exposed the leader's discomfort with it, and should more properly be seen as a device for avoiding having to even struggle with the subject of leadership.) Somewhat more promisingly, experiential or academically derived theories of leadership sometimes were found to have been consciously developed and applied. Unfortunately, they consistently fell short of the mark, operated in a peculiarly irrelevant fashion within the organization, or were actively harmful to the organization's effectiveness and ability to pursue its aim. Graduate, postgraduate, and focused professional study of the topic has not alleviated my concern. Rather, most of this study has exacerbated that concern, and led to a conviction that much of what has been done in the field has not only led us off the mark, but has contributed to the leadership crises we are experiencing today.

This book will argue that the modern school of individual leadership has failed to grasp the true nature of organizational leadership. In turn, this leadership movement has led astray the leaders it purports to coach, as well as their organizations and all of those who depend upon them. In some cases, the results have been not only unfortunate, but spectacularly so. In all cases, however, I believe that the focus on the individual leader at the top creates unsustainable burdens and pressures on that person. These erode the ability to maintain perspective and safeguard the proper relationships between the modern senior executive and the organization. The result, at a minimum, is inconsistent and generally inferior levels of productivity in virtually every plane of organizational functioning.

The argument will be made that leadership in an organization is in no wise an individual characteristic, and certainly not a characteristic of any particular individual. While it is expressed through individuals, it is itself an innate quality of the joining together of numbers of people in a collaborative effort in an organizational setting. It arises from, communicates itself among, and is expressed through all members of the organization in varying degrees according to the general level of group cohesion in the organization, and the abilities and circumstances at any given time of the individuals concerned. Thus, it is potentially more comprehensive and powerful an asset for the organization than the leadership generated by any individual leader, however capable such a person might be.

The management of this organizational leadership thus serves a number of purposes. It relieves the senior executive of the untenable burdens and expectations of individual leadership that he has assumed, or that have been placed upon him. It obviates and reverses the erosion of the integrity of the organization that arises when its focus is misdirected from its purpose to that of its leader. In addition, it makes available to the intelligently managed organization a source of leadership that is potentially far more powerful. The key is in recognizing what it is, and learning how to bring it into the service of the organization.

This book, then, aims to present a new view of what organizational leadership really is, and how to manage it. In so doing, it is hoped that management will reclaim its natural supremacy over leadership in an organizational setting. Further, the book is a call to raise our organizations out of the thralldom to individual leadership into which they have fallen, and to restore them to intelligent, responsible, owner-focused management.

Who this book was written for

The intended audience of this book is not merely the practicing manager. I certainly do hope that managers will learn much from the book and be encouraged to use it to help them manage more effectively and efficiently. However, it is targeted at a larger audience. It is hoped that corporate and other organizational boards will learn to use the book to help them regain control over their organizations. The quasi-cult of the modern charismatic leader has led to various mechanisms that have shifted the balance in the management-ownership relationship out of equilibrium. This has further led to an erosion of organizational integrity and of the usefulness of both management and owners to their organizations. One of the aims of this book is to redraw the profile of the senior executive from singular leader to effective manager, and thus to help restore that equilibrium.

I hope, as well, that the book will receive critical attention in business schools and the large leadership consulting industry. I believe that it is important for this topic to be debated vigorously, and to be opened to the healthy and robust reexamination of assumptions that have gone unchallenged for far too long. There have been suggestions, some quite broad, in the literature since at least the early 20th century, that point in the direction of the argument taken in this book. I think it would be useful for professional practitioners, scholars, and observers to turn their attention to a reassessment of that line of leadership commentary.

Organization of the book

The introductory Part I contains three chapters that present the case for the need for this book. The first chapter challenges the nature of the contributions of the modern leadership movement and provides an overview of the movement's lack of cohesiveness, suggesting that this may indicate a measure of questionable verisimilitude. Chapter 2 provides a closer look at some of the more dominant and rising influences in the modern leadership movement—and how they might be contributing to the problem. Finally, Chapter 3 goes a little deeper into the recent and more distant history of the literature to find and discuss those hints buried within it that offer glimmers of promise pointing in the direction of the argument of this book.

Part II consists of four chapters that lay out the argument for the existence of organizational leadership, and for the ability and importance of intelligently managing it. Chapter 4 builds upon observations, made in another context, of the behavior of soldiers in combat units. These are then used as a basis upon which to draw our own more general observations about organizational behavior and leadership. The discussion here builds the basis for what follows. The next chapter extends those observations to begin building the case for the existence of organizational leadership. It does this principally by showing how leadership can occur at various times and points throughout an organization. Chapter 6 then presents the full case for organizational leadership—what it is and how it operates in an organization. Chapter 7 closes the main part of the book with a discussion of how to manage organizational leadership.

The concluding Part III consists of two chapters, beginning with the presentation of possible critiques of the book's arguments. Certainly, the ideas proposed herein about leadership are not in the commonly adhered-to tradition of the topic. These ideas may be difficult to absorb, and will likely attract resistance for disturbing what have been apparently satisfactory habits of thought. Accordingly,

I have attempted, in this chapter, to anticipate several of these critiques made from several perspectives, and to persuasively address them. The final chapter offers a concise review of the argument of the book, although the reader should be cautioned that it is not a self-contained substitute for the broader argumentation made in Part II. It then concludes with some thoughts about how to proceed with implementation of the concepts presented.

A note on usage

It should be useful here to discuss how some vocabulary and general usage has been employed in this book. To begin with, I have consciously chosen to use the male gender as a general stand-in for third-party references to people or human society. I should like to note here that while I have found that there are indeed differences in the general tendencies and approaches of men and women to management, the topic is a complex one that can only be very tangentially addressed here. First, these differences admit of numerous exceptions that, while not compromising their validity as generalizations, do make it rather impractical to thoughtlessly project them onto particular individuals or situations. Second, I have found that the differing natural strengths of women and men are complementary and are in fact quite powerful in combination. In fact, while it is not common, neither is it unheard of to see people, male and female, who have developed and unified these strengths within themselves, with results for managerial effectiveness that generally leave others in a state of baffled admiration. Third, while a discussion of these issues is not appropriate here and will not be attempted, I should say that I do not believe that the natural strengths of one sex are necessarily or inherently superior to the other. Still, if pressed, I would have to say that, all other factors being equal, the average organization would be best served not by an individual male or female (unless one is a unifier of the strengths of both sexes), nor even by a male/female team, but rather by a female executive with key male subordinates. Again, this is not intended as a reflection of the superiority of one set of strengths over the other, but merely of where those natural strengths are best placed to provide the greatest combined service to the organization. Further, it admits of as many validating exceptions as does the basic generalization. Nevertheless, regarding third party references in this book, I ask your forbearance for my use of the male gender in a general sense, to avoid the inelegant and distracting circumlocutions that are sometimes used to mollify rather than to enlighten.

I often refer to owners in this book, which is about all types of organizations, and not just corporations or other business units. The term *owner* refers to any person or legal entity that has owner-level authority and responsibility for the creation and direction of the organization. In addition to shareholders, this can refer to foundations and governmental institutions that take a similar originating and fundamental interest role. Similarly, I use the terms *boards*, *boards of directors*, and *directors* to refer to intermediary persons or bodies legitimately delegated owner-level authority and responsibility comparable to that of a corporate board.

The heart of this book is the discussion of leaders and leadership. However, these words themselves admit of a wide range of usage that can lead to confusion. As a general rule, I will use the term *leader* as a quasi-technical reference to the sort of individual promoted by the modern leadership movement as uniquely suited by natural character, character training, leadership training, or any combination of these, for leadership of an organization. *Leadership* is generally used together with *individual* or *charismatic* to refer to what such individuals do. When used together with *organizational*, however, it refers to the concept of leadership propounded in this book.

Furthermore, *leaders* and *leadership* are used herein with reference to organizations and their activities. They are not to be confused with the use of these words in describing historical trends, market positions, technological innovation, or the like. As used in this book, the terms refer to professional executives employed to run an organization. When they are used to refer to owners, explorers, adventurers in various endeavors, or to refer to the relative standing of entities compared to others at a given point in time, they take on meanings that, while perfectly legitimate in those contexts, are not relevant to their use in this book.

It is my intent to describe in this book what I believe to be a perfectly ordinary, comprehensible, and manageable organizational asset. Mindful of Samuel Clemens's comment that if he had had more time, he would have written a shorter book, I have attempted to be respectfully concise and succinct. I hope nevertheless that you will have been provided sufficient argumentation of my case to take away from your reading of it ideas that will be of meaningful use to you in your endeavors, whatever they may be. I further hope that whatever views you form of the ideas presented in this book, you will be encouraged to promote additional discussion of them by others. Such a debate will make more robust and usefully enduring our understanding and application of whatever ideas emerge from it. Finally, I will be very pleased to find that you have enjoyed and benefited from the time you spend with this book.

PART I
Introduction

When I began to talk with him,
I could not help thinking that he was not really wise,
although he was thought wise by many,
and still wiser by himself;

…

I am better off than he is—for he knows nothing and thinks that he knows.
I neither know nor think that I know.
In this latter particular, then, I seem to have slightly the advantage of him.

…

After this I went to one man after another

…

I found that the men most in repute were all but the most foolish;
and that some inferior men were really wiser and better.

Plato's Socrates, in *The Apology*

1

What's Happened

"The people cannot see him enough. They delight in a man.
Here is a head and a trunk! What a front! What eyes!
Atlantean shoulders, and the whole carriage heroic,
with equal inward force to guide the great machine!"

—Ralph Waldo Emerson

The last few decades of the 20th century witnessed an explosion of interest in the subject of leadership. Academic and general-interest writing on the topic became widely popular. New ideas were insufficient to the need, and old sources, from Sun-Tzu through Attila the Hun to Machiavelli, were pressed back into service to close the breach. Alongside cults and apocalyptic groups warning of the dangers at hand with the close of the old millennium, there arose a plethora of leadership centers and gurus heralding the exciting possibilities appearing with the dawn of the new one. We learned that a special sort of ill-understood being was needed to confront the dizzying changes and challenges befalling us at every turn—only these "leaders" were capable of guiding us through such perilous and confusing times.

However, before long, as always, our democratic instincts rebelled against this elitist view of the leader. We began to have explained to us that leadership derives not from nature, but from nurture. It is a learned set of skills. As this particular nature versus nurture debate progressed, we came to understand that alongside the child within each of us is a leader as well. The issue is how to give expression to that aspect of our character.

Through this device, the elitists and democrats, the advocates of nature and of nurture, could all claim some portion of victory. Leadership is both special and within the reach of all of us. It is both inherent and learned.

The result has been a bewildering array of theories of leadership, all promising to offer the vital insight that will unlock the secrets of this remarkable skill and make it accessible to all of us. These have been developed from grave and ponderously scientific academic studies, or from interviews of present-day leaders. Some have been built up from surveys of "great men" throughout history. Still others are derived from studies of organizations that have shown some quantifiable measures of success.

But the question bears asking: If we have called up this frenzied discussion of leadership in order to produce leaders to guide us through these presumed historically unique times of change, how are they doing? Whether these leaders are a result of all the activity and theorizing in the field, or whether all of that theorizing is a result of studies of these leaders, where have they led us? And what has happened to us in the meanwhile?

It is not necessary here to provide a detailed accounting of the scandals that have rocked the business world in the late 1990s and early 2000s. Industries have been broken, wealth destroyed, dreams shattered. Many presumably revolutionary new industries turned out to be exaggerated adaptations of traditional ones. The market swelled with the entry of millions of small investors, either directly or indirectly, through mutual funds or company retirement plans. When the bubble burst, a staggering amount of their money simply vanished. People had believed what they were told by the leaders of this business revolution, leaders who were advertised as able to see what others could not, who were guiding us through dangerous times to a grand new world beyond. These people invested their retirement contributions in these visions. Millions of them were then left unable to retire: they were told by these leaders to have faith, and they did.

In many cases these workers not only can't retire, but they are left holding the bag, struggling to keep their crippled, ill-conceived businesses afloat. At the same time, it appears that those leaders, evidently less sanguine about the veracity of their own leadership skills than they encouraged their followers to be, were able to jump to safety with carefully pre-packed golden parachutes. Many of these businesses will not make it. However, those leaders, who promised they would make it, are well protected both legally and financially. Perhaps they did have pretty good foresight, after all.

Similar stories can be told about the condition of leadership in governments across the United States: scandal, bankruptcy, failing infrastructure, whole jurisdictions seemingly drifting helplessly toward disaster. Why do Americans spend so much and provide such poor education to their children? Why are some states approaching financial collapse? What will America's political leaders do to the promises made to the country's social security beneficiaries, many of whom have little else to rely on in old age, having lost their retirement plans to the empty promises of their business leaders?

As it happens, leaders, while enjoying the rewards of their successes, rarely suffer the consequences of their failures. The moral jeopardy that results lays the basis for further scandal and failure. Governments then step in to attempt to regulate accountability into the system. How did this result from such an intense period of leadership studies and promotion of styles and models for addressing just such times as these?

It is difficult to avoid the observation that the striking increase in leadership studies and education in the 1980s and 1990s corresponded with—or culminated in—spectacular leadership failures. To what extent is the one a result of the other? How and why did this happen? What is to be done about it?

This book will argue that the inflated promises of the leadership movement are indeed culpable in the disastrous leadership failures that have occurred in both business and government, both in the US and around the world. By identifying leadership as an individual characteristic, the movement distorted and diminished the proper managerial functions of the executive. By placing exaggerated promise in the vision and inspirational duties of the individual leader, the movement gave undue power and license to that individual. Further, it encouraged the "followers" to place their faith in and abandon their judgment to this momentous personage. All the associated commentary about morality and "knowing the self" could not relieve the resulting burdens thus placed on the leader—rather, it exacerbated them. All the heroic expectations currently placed on the leadership abilities of senior executives often lead to distorted and grandiose perceptions of them by themselves and others. This, in turn, can lead to an oracular administration emitting cryptic messages from the sheltered leader, which are then interpreted and transmitted to the benighted masses by an elite priesthood of senior executives. The results can vary from rather unpredictable successes to rather more predictable failures—although, in either event, they tend to be reliably spectacular and epic. Curiously, it can become difficult to fix accountability in such circumstances. In addition, that can produce great pressures and temptations for the taking of great and unwarranted risks—legal or otherwise.

What can be done about it? Actually, it is a quite manageable problem, as will be seen. First, however, we will take a closer look at why it is necessary.

DEFINITIONS

Leadership as a separate discipline has proved notoriously difficult to distinguish, and there is no consensus for a single definition. Each new theory or model is generally accompanied by its own description of what leadership is. Over time, this has resulted in a multitude of mutually irreconcilable definitions that have badly fragmented the subject area and rendered it difficult to navigate. In virtually every new discussion of leadership, it is necessary first to establish and agree to the intellectual framework to be used, and then to the associated definitions of terms. The disputes arising from this process fruitlessly expend much energy of the sort that produces more heat than light. Little agreement is reached among the disputants, and even less clarity is provided the observers.

Moreover, when the dust settles, one finds by the side of the field, the definition of management, badly mugged. Its pockets have been picked of any elements of value relating to leadership. It has been so badly abused that it no longer represents a particularly inspiring or worthwhile human endeavor. The manager has been reduced to a mere maintenance technician. However, the attempt to break out the role of leadership from the duties of management has weakened the latter institution without successfully establishing the former. As in so many such precipitous hit and run fads, the victim is indeed damaged, but the pickpocket is unable to convert the stolen goods into anything of real value.

Instead, we are left with intriguing sounding slogans about what grand things leaders do in contrast to what mundane things managers do. On closer examination, however, these slogans bear no sustainably positive message about leadership; they merely blame—or at least belittle—the victimized manager. Thus, we eagerly greet each new definition, each new model, until the bubble bursts. In the end, we are left with precious little of the promised leadership, and with a badly weakened managerial discipline.

How did this come about?

For the better part of the modern period, the affairs of industrial-age societies were directed largely by a command and control style of management. This was sufficient to meet the challenges and innovations that were developed through most of this period.

However, in the 20th century in the US, the pace of change began to pick up speed. More large, complex, and consumer-oriented—or at least consumer-aware—organizations appeared. For example, Ford Motor Company created a manufacturing process, and associated management techniques, in order to provide inexpensive automobiles to a previously unserved market. Later, General

Motors organized itself, and its management systems, in order to serve the segments appearing in the broader market, as well as their changing tastes.

After World War II, large numbers of men, who had learned to manage and participate in great and large-scale enterprises, returned from military duty and received university educations under the GI Bill. Partly due to the powerful stimulus of their reentry, the economy grew, the supply and demand sides of the markets both became more sophisticated, and innovations multiplied to meet increasing demands for quality and specialization. Concern grew that traditional methods of organizing enterprises were no longer sufficient to the need. As time progressed, the perceived shock grew of the future seeming to arrive in unexpected ways with increasing frequency and velocity. Even the newly professionalized discipline of management was deemed too shortsighted to deal with this dizzying pace of change. Great new companies, and even industries, were being created. Traditional organizations seemed to be foundering like dinosaurs bewildered by the changing of the epochs. We could no longer manage our progress into, and our engagement with, the future. We needed leaders who could somehow see further down the road, who could develop a vision of what we needed to be or do to meet that future, and who could teach and inspire us to develop the flexibility and agility needed to come to grips with it.

Initially, models of this different sort of executive were found in the military. Military engagements are famously befogged with frictions of all sorts. It is widely acknowledged that it can take a special kind of genius—of inspired and exalted individual leadership—to produce clear victory from such formidably destructive confusion. Business leaders were compared with such leaders, and business and military history were scoured to produce and analyze such examples. The growing field of leadership studies and training attracted great interest, particularly during the 1980s and 1990s. Adjustments of traditional ideas and new insights and concepts were developed to attract attention, disciples, and business for a growing number of leadership consultants, training centers, and writers.

The only source of authority for the new role of the executive leader, however, was in the traditional executive manager's job description. As a result, it was simply taken away, leaving the manager to putter around the machinery and handle the organization's hygiene functions. It became the role of the new executive leader to breathe the spark of life into the organization's body, to invest it with faith, and to lead it into the promised land of the future.

As the leadership movement attracted interest from the business world, various contenders for the resulting business laid claim to the secrets of that spark of life. Yet, none of their definitions have proven decisively authentic; they, and ever increasing new ones, continue to jostle for supremacy. Thus, as mentioned, there are numerous definitions that are difficult to unify.

Even general definitions are difficult to agree upon. Some limit the **basic definition of leadership** to setting direction and communicating it. Others add wording that implies certain organizational tasks; one even supposes that it does not exist unless the followers are held responsible for their actions—a most unpromising development for the movement.

Definitions that are more specific can be grouped by the general approach that they take to the topic. For example, the general view of the so-called traditional directive style of leadership is often referred to as the **authority model**. In this view, the leaders are followed because they have been given the legitimate authority to lead. According to the sociologist Max Weber, this can take the following forms: 1) **rational-legal**—this accrues to the occupant of an office which holds the actual authority; 2) **traditional**—this arises simply from habit or customary practice; and 3) **charismatic**—this type of leadership authority is drawn to those with special characteristics.

The latter has led to various types of theory, which are built on special features of the individual leader. Examples of these theories are **charismatic authority**, **great man theory,** and **trait theory**. All of these define leadership as the expression of special characteristics or traits that are possessed by particular people, who thus command rare abilities to inspire others and to attract broad followings. While no distinct set of such peculiar traits or characteristics has been shown to actually exist among putative leaders, the theories continue to attract attention.

A quite different view was developed from the 1950s to the 1970s. **Contingency theory**—sometimes referred to as **situational theory**—proposed the notion that leadership is a fluid concept that should be adapted to each situation in which it takes place. For example, a Detroit automobile manufacturing plant should be led differently than a Hollywood film-production company. The psychologist Rensis Likert developed a well-known approach in which he identified four systems which he felt described how leaders led in varying situations: 1) **exploitative/authoritative**, 2) **benevolent/authoritative**, 3) **consultative**, and 4) **participative**.

In the midst of this period, in 1960, Douglas McGregor presented **Theory X** and **Theory Y**. Theory X described a leadership model built on the assumption that people are naturally lazy and must be disciplined and closely supervised in order to get any work out of them. It is what is often imagined as the typical authoritarian leadership style. Theory Y is a model based on the opposite assumption, arguing that adults have a natural desire to seek fulfillment through productive work. It builds on this to describe a system that integrates the interests and motivations of the organization and the workers. While many organizations took either of these theories to be applicable according to the maturity or level of development of the work team or organizational culture, McGregor himself believed Theory X to be wholly inappropriate in any circumstance; he strongly encouraged adoption of the Theory Y philosophy. It should be noted that, in an effort to address criticisms of his previous work, McGregor later began work on a **Theory Z**, but died before it was completed. William Ouichi wrote a book by that title, expanding on and further promoting McGregor's Theory Y organizational philosophy.

The academic approach of viewing human behavior specifically from actions and behavior, rather than personality, is referred to as behaviorism. Thinkers from this discipline reacted to what they believed to be an impractical and fruitless focus on the individual leader's characteristics. These writers began to develop their ideas in the 1970s, well before the modern leadership movement really took off. In the early 1970s, a British theorist named John Adair proposed a behaviorist model of leadership, which he called **Action-Centered Leadership**. It is based on three principal activities he identified as performed by leaders: 1) build and maintain teams, 2) accomplish the task, and 3) develop individuals. However, others in the behaviorist movement criticized this model as too simplistic.

Eager to qualify as properly less accessible to the rest of us, many such complex theories were developed. However, even within the same discipline, a good number of them conflicted with each other. One of the better-known examples from this school is referred to as the **managerial grid**, a product of the consulting industry. This measures a leader against two scales—concern for task and concern for people. It defines the resulting leadership style based on where the measures of these two scales intersect in a matrix.

In the late 1970s, James MacGregor Burns developed the **transactional theory of leadership** and the **transformational theory of leadership**. They both suggest that there is an exchange of value between leaders and followers. However, in transactional leadership the exchange is of tangible things—measurable production for salary, for example. In transformational leadership, the exchange is in moral values—the leaders and followers raise each other to higher levels of motivation and morality. Certain of the new breed of organizational psychologists are clearer about who is being transformed—it is the follower. A recent study of transformational leadership as exhibited in US Army units claims that the leader's orders are not designed merely to take soldiers from point A to point B, but to have produced an improved soldier in the course of the journey.

The **power and influence theory** suggests that leadership is built upon the interrelationships of people in an organization. These interrelationships are formed around the structure provided by the power and influence generated by the leader. The generation of these is the leader's more or less direct contribution. The particular form of leadership and followership employed in the organization arises from the nature of those interrelationships, and thus are a secondary influence of the individual leader.

Another theory from psychology argues that leaders observe their followers and attempt to determine what causes their behavior under various circumstances. Having determined to what they can attribute their followers' behavior, the leaders then form specific approaches to exploit that discovery in ways that produce desired behavior. This is known as the **attribution theory of leadership**.

These are the some of the principal precursors and important influences on the modern leadership movement's views of leadership. While such approaches will be critiqued in the next chapter, it is useful to say here that they at least have the virtue of attempting, generally, to be descriptive. They are based on observations, studies, and surveys. They try to explain what exists. Their prescriptive content, while present (a notable example is the management grid), is secondary. The modern movement of the latter 20th century and early years of the 21st is marked by prescriptive and exhortative approaches to leadership. As such, they do not so much have definitions, in the ordinary sense of the word, of leadership; they have aspirations for it. Moreover, as they have proliferated, they have provided a great and diverse field of leadership terms. A review of these will serve to lay the groundwork for the next chapter.

TERMS

The principal leadership theories and studies have generated a special language with its own terminology. Many of these terms gain currency through coverage of the main models in university course work, and are widely used in the general business-related press. For example, *Theory X, Theory Y, and* the *Great Man Theory* are commonly understood and even self-evident references to the appropriate theories. Of course, this common category of terms includes *leaders, natural leaders, transactional leaders, transformational leaders,* and *followers.*

There are related terms such as *groups, Great Groups,* and *teams*—even *membership organizations.* As a complement to leadership, followers have attracted efforts to develop a model of *followership.* In the shouldering and bustling for preeminence in the burgeoning leadership movement, however, the real prize is in innovative insights into what leadership really is—or what it ought to be. Accordingly, many ingenious versions of the term now litter the field.

For example, it seems that even real leaders should not be complacent, but should aspire to the next level of excellence, which is the *agent of change.* If you prefer, there is the noble *servant leader,* who works to improve the community and the workplace (not to increase profit). There is the *conscious leader,* who leads people toward themselves. For the more traditional-minded, there are *results-based leaders.* On the other hand, there are also *visionary, fulfillment,* and *integration leaders.* There are *coercive, authoritative, affiliative, democratic, pacesetting,* and *coaching leaders. Primal leaders* display what is known as emotional intelligence, which is intended to describe traits that seem to be better predictors of success than mere raw intelligence.

One of the more engagingly democratic concepts is that of an organization filled with *leaderful people.* However, perhaps the most disorientingly creative term describes those who lead us into future realities not discernible by we mere mortals; these are the *edgewalkers.*

Some psychologists are attempting to connect the concepts of creativity and leadership; developing a category they call *creative leadership.* Leaders, in this view, can be categorized in a variety of ways, according to how they use their creativity in their leadership roles. For example, *replicators* protect the status quo. *Redefiners,* on the other hand, add a new twist to an ordinary idea. *Forward incrementors* advance an organization a step forward in the direction it is already heading, and *advanced forward incrementors* make a daring leap forward. *Redirectors* take the organization in a wholly new direction. *Regressive redirectors* reinstitute an older concept into the present context. *Reinitiators* give new life to an organization that appears to have been losing its energy or innovativeness. Finally, *synthesizers* integrate concepts from various fields into a new idea. The people advancing these notions tend to confuse various meanings of the word *leader.* For example, they compare a composer who is not appreciated in his own time with organizational leaders. This is a common error. It equates the status or attainment of developmental, technical, market, artistic, or some such form of leadership, with the job of managing an organization. Leadership, in the former sense, merely denotes an advanced position in a particular field at a particular time; it does not reflect possession of the ability to lead a collaborative enterprise. Nevertheless, one of the lessons these theorists draw from such comparisons is that leaders should not be concerned with attracting approval; they should be willing to do what is unpopular—even condemned—if it is a pure expression of their creativity. It does not seem, however, to be a very practical idea to encourage modern organizational leaders to cultivate condemnation of their actions, or to measure the success of their methods by the degree to which they are rejected by the community or the board. Nevertheless, these thinkers go further, and recommend that boards or bosses actually select various of these types of leaders according to the needs of the moment. For example, a *redirector* is argued as the best choice for an organization that is stagnant and needs to be shaken up. Then, presumably, some form of *incrementor* should take over. Organizations are expected to switch out leaders as circumstances, and their directors' understanding of the organization's needs, change over time. We are to suppose that there is a bench of suitably categorized leaders who can be sent into the game, and then benched again, whenever the coach (whoever that is) deems that to be appropriate.

Peculiar examples such as that in the preceding paragraph certainly do little to clarify our understanding of organizational leadership. On the other hand, the more ordinary and general attempts to define leadership, discussed earlier in this chapter, have their own problems. Among them is the unavoidable conclusion that the modern understanding of the field of leadership has been pilfered from the definition of management. Definitions from this more recent element of the leadership movement are only able to describe leadership as being "about" something. This is then contrasted with what management is (or is defined down to be). Alternatively, the description of individual leadership is comparative, such as when it is depicted as "more" proactive, or people-oriented, or the like, than is management.

Naturally, there are complex discussions, in this element of the leadership movement, of the characteristics of leaders and of the sorts of things they do. Such discussions actually get down to the central problems with this modern movement's prescriptions; they will be dealt with in the next chapter.

2

What's Wrong

"Sincerity is the most important asset in life;
if you can fake that, you've got it made."

—Groucho Marx

Leadership has been a topic of study throughout recorded history. From Plutarch to Machiavelli, students of the subject have attempted to discover, describe, and promote competing theories of political and military leadership. With the rise of large non-governmental organizations in the 20th century, attention gradually shifted toward them. As their roles in and effect on society increased in prominence, they began to attract scholarly activity. Studies were conducted that were, basically, descriptive in nature and that were conducted primarily by academics and professional observers. As organizations became more complex and differentiated, the management consulting industry developed and became increasingly sophisticated in serving them. The industry grew to offer specialized expertise in various areas of organizational strategy, development, finance, operations, and specific areas of management. Toward the end of the century, leadership became one of these specialties—even an industry in its own right.

The leadership consulting industry commissioned surveys and studies to help meet demand for the product—and to help legitimize it. The uncertainty of the rapidly changing and increasingly competitive business environment, combined with highly effective and novel marketing, led to surging demand. This led, in turn, to surging supply. New entrants sought ways to attract market share by differentiating their product, applying niche-marketing techniques, or seeking out entirely new markets. The industry grew beyond the borders of the traditional consulting industry, which included leadership studies and consulting as a part of its overall product portfolio, to encompass small outfits and individuals specializing wholly in the field.

The subject had crossed an important threshold. Previously, it had been a field of analysis and commentary by scholars and professional observers. While these may have expressed preferences, their work was largely descriptive of existing and emerging trends, and explored how various scientific disciplines might illuminate the subject. Now, however, it has become a product for development and sale by specialized market researchers and consultants. Research has evolved from examining what is the case, to examining what can be sold. The product itself has come to be more prescriptive—even exhortative. It has become directed at the concerns of a wide variety of "stakeholders," rather than of owners and managers. New models have come to be described with reference to sales features, such as needs, advantages, benefits, and costs.

Once leadership became a business, the dynamics of business altered its nature fundamentally. As supply burgeoned, the product splintered and took on multiple forms according to the segmentation of the market, means of product delivery, and fashion, which changed as the overall market expanded and matured. Innovation became meaningless, as it was increasingly driven by the needs of the product's suppliers, rather than its consumers. It further had the unfortunate effect of promoting a cult-like approach to leadership and individual leaders. These "innovations" will be examined in two general groupings: 1) the uniqueness of leadership and 2) the democratization of leadership.

CONCENTRATING ON THE LEADER

The modern leadership movement can be viewed as consisting of two main groups. One believes that leaders possess special characteristics that, while nominally within the grasp of all, are, in fact, not generally attained by the rest of us. This group is concerned with identifying these characteristics, describing the leaders who possess them, and elaborating the role of these leaders in their organizations.

However, by placing such emphasis on the role of the individual leader and his (or her) unique characteristics, the movement creates expectations for him (or her) that generally cannot be met. From the perspective of this group's general framework, the fate of the entire organization can appear to be tied up in the special qualities of the individual anointed to lead it. This leads to both an overdependence of the organization on the individual leader, and a separation of the individual leader from the organization. In fact, it can sometimes appear that the organization's principal role is merely to serve as a vehicle for expression of the leader's leadership. On top of all this, this school of leadership has set into motion an unfolding of events that tends to culminate in the debilitation of the organization's board.

While many current thinkers on leadership find it obligatory to declare that becoming a leader is within the reach of everyone, upon doing so, they move right along to place oracle-like burdens on these leaders. Leaders are described with reference to personal characteristics that confer on them special abilities for perceiving and attaining success. A peculiar feature of these discussions is a focus on the leader with little more than passing reference to the organization or its other members. When such reference is made, it often appears to not be genuinely directed at attempting to understand or describe their roles, but simply for the purpose of amplifying points being made about the individual leader.

The modern leadership movement literature typically focuses on what are generally depicted as four core leadership characteristics. These can be summarized as the abilities to deal with change, rally others behind a goal, adhere to a moral compass, and to know one's self. Many leadership writers describe these as the essential core characteristics of a leader. It should be noted, however, that none of the characteristics actually references an organization. Only one refers to followers, but this is typically done in order to emphasize the unique abilities of the leader in contrast to the followers. Some writers note that these are core characteristics that are necessary in any leadership setting, but that additional industry-specific skills and knowledge would be required in particular positions. This, however, still ignores the organization and places the emphasis for leadership and its unique contributions directly on the leader's shoulders. Further, failing to provide a context for leadership (such as corporate goals and the organization designed to attain them), such discussions, having nowhere else to go, are inevitably driven further back into the individual.

The One Constant

Consider the first characteristic, which deals with change. Discussions in this area vary from describing the leader as one who has unique individual hardiness and resilience enabling him to cope with change, to one who possesses the special courage to dissent, to challenge the status quo, and to force change. The problem with this is that such capabilities, in and of themselves, are not only not particularly rare or important, but that, in the absence of context, they can be unproductive and disruptive—even dangerous. The discussion, however, tends to create a sense of chaos in the environment and an urgency that the matter must be addressed by he who has the courage and the ability to do so; the turmoil can only be penetrated by the unique personal insight, skill, toughness, and courage of the individual leader. That is to say, change is something the leader must see and to effect—not something that may or may not be an issue for the organization. The result is that pressure is put on leaders to exhibit these characteristics and to create activity—even to generate change—in the absence of context.

Follow the Leader

The ability to inspire followers to rally behind one's leadership also tends to be discussed in the absence of organizational context. The topic attracts an inordinate and almost celebratory focus on the leader's ability to generate enthusiastic followers. This discussion tends to take place with respect to the creation of goals that inspire followership. Further, the goals developed by leaders are not the ordinary sort; rather, they are often characterized as elevated and special—even, as a prominent leadership guru has put it, comparable to "a mission from God." While there is nothing particularly wrong with development of goals so lofty, there may not be anything especially necessary or worthwhile about it either. The unique concern, here, is that goal generation is described as a function of the leader, rather than as a requirement of the organization. Leaders display leadership by creating ambitious and uplifting goals. The goals give expression to the leader's leadership—not to the purpose of the organization.

Walk this Way

Related to the ability to generate followership is the sense among the followers that the leader can be trusted. The other side of that coin is that the leader must not abuse the trust placed in him. This topic is generally discussed in the framework of morality, or the possession by the leader of a system of principles—a moral compass.

However, to discuss morality as a uniquely necessary characteristic of a leader is to pile yet more messianic hype on the role of this singular individual. The consequences of such an exalted image can often be less than ennobling. The fact is that everyone needs a moral compass. The issue of morality among those in authority in an organization is one, not of leadership, but of *command*. Those who issue orders or instructions that others are obliged to follow would do well for themselves, the organization, and its members—and, in particular, for its owners—if they possessed such an instrument. However, the uniqueness of the need for this tool, in this context, is to help guide those who possess both command authority and fiduciary duties—not to enable them to discharge the functions of leadership.

The real meaning of the discussion of morality when applied to leadership relates to the previous one of followership. If it is true that people follow better those in whom they have faith and confidence, then it follows that a moral compass is a necessary element of a leader's toolkit. It extends the faith in the leader through times when the logic of his or her demands may be difficult to discern, or even that the rightness of them may be doubted, were it not for the unquestioned moral stature of the leader asking them of us. One leadership guru summarizes this topic, with perhaps inadvertent frankness, by averring that credibility is the most important characteristic of a leader. What is important, then, is simply to be believable.

Morality in the context of social enterprises is too important a human characteristic to be imputed to one person. However, as mentioned, in certain circumstances it is especially important to have faith that it is possessed by he whose commands we must follow without question. There are not many of these circumstances outside of war; nevertheless, in those rare cases where we are gripped by uncertainty, fear, and the urgent and unavoidable need to act, special care must indeed have been taken that our commanders' morals are not an item we need concern ourselves with. In the more ordinary world of organizational life, we should be less concerned with the morality of those in authority than with our own. Those senior executives who lack morality are not likely to obtain it simply because it is on someone's list of requirements for leaders. What such individuals need is checks and balances, not the removal of these in order to enhance their freedom to act, relying on an inappropriate, and far too often misplaced, faith in the unimpeachable purity of their characters.

Journey to the Center of the Ego

Possibly the most frequently commented on leadership characteristic is the apparently unique need for a leader to possess self-knowledge. If we have not heretofore seen enough evidence of the dangerous emphasis on the special character of the single individual vested with the mantle of leadership, then perhaps this is it.

Leaders are encouraged to learn who they really are, how they think, how they are affected by events and by others, and how events and others are affected by them. They need to discover what matters to them and what really doesn't, what agitates them, what engages their ingenuity and creativity, and what is of no moment to them.

It is incumbent on them to undertake a journey of self-discovery that leads them to finding the deep wells of judgment, courage, and wisdom that will help them give voice to their personal leadership. In the end, they will emerge from this profound spiritual trek to take up their mission in the world. It is important, however, to return to the mountain regularly, to replenish the spirit, and to drink again from one's unique springs of inspiration.

Such navel-pondering narcissism all too often encourages a desperate lack of perspective. As commonly found in the literature, the emphasis is on the singularity of the leader and his rare and vital gifts, not on the organization and its purposes and resources. It is about the contributor, not the contribution. Far from placing the leader's role and characteristics in context and integrating them with his responsibilities, such discussions further isolate the leader from the organization. The organization becomes his charge, his tribe, often headstrong and rebellious, for him to lead, relying on the inner resources that he has discovered during his spiritual journey, and that he continuously revives and renews.

A philosophy of individual leadership that places such celebratory adulation at the feet of the singular individual that it has wrapped in the prophetic robes of leadership can lead only to the destruction of that individual, as well as of those who have become dependent on him. The stress is too great. No one, however intelligent, moral, or persevering, can bear the extraordinary and unrelenting pressure.

Too much responsibility is placed on the leader, and too little on the organization and its owners. This leads to a separation of the leader from the organization that he was presumably appointed to lead. His policies and decisions are evaluated based on his personal characteristics of creativity and courage, rather than on the more mundane standards of the organization, its purpose, and its operating circumstances.

In an environment of excessive regard for—even obeisance to—the rare characteristics of an individual leader, attention tends to stray from the needs of the organization—to which the leader was initially appointed to attend—to the needs of the leader. Indeed, the organization is often re-examined with respect to its ability to act on the leader's guidance. One leadership guru goes so far as to say that the organization should be designed and managed in such a way as to most efficiently enable it to give expression to the "inspired musings" emanating from the visionary leader.

Completing the oracular image is the school of leadership that describes leaders as edgewalkers. In this school of thought, the leader is possessed of a kind of inspired genius that periodically seizes him and causes him to issue forth visions of the future. This personage is consciously characterized as a modern corporate version of the ancient village shaman, serving as a sort of window into the future, sensing and interpreting visions thereof for those of us mired in the present. The leader is described as a right-brain intuitive; when asked how he knows what he knows, he can only answer cryptically, "I just know." He walks on the leading edge, where we dare not tread, and he has the courage to act on what he sees from there and is able to communicate to us. We are encouraged to have faith in the leader's supernatural ability—to be willing to organize our actions, and our very enterprises, around the presumed veracity of his visions, for the very reason that he cannot defend that veracity in terms understandable to us.

This kind of writing encourages the sort of irresponsible self-absorption that caters to those whose egos are likely of sufficient girth as it is. It supports the argument that these leaders have special abilities not accessible to the rest of us. Our obligation—all of us, whether owner, partner, employee, supplier or even customer—is merely to suspend judgment and to accept, with humility and gratitude, the gift of leadership offered us. It is a frank completion of the argument that the modern leader's rights must be de-coupled from his responsibilities.

The inordinate faith placed in, or expectations made of, the abilities of such leaders leads to shifts in attitude and structure within the organization and its owners. These shifts gradually place the organization and its owners in far too dependent a relationship with—if not in thrall to—the leader. The traditional administrator/organization relationship is distorted. The emphasis shifts, sometimes imperceptibly, from the executive serving the organization's requirements, to the organization finding itself compelled to serve the leader's requirements. The questions from within the organization and among its observers begin to revolve around, not what the organization itself needs or is doing, but what the leader wants and is planning. Instead of examining what actions the leader is taking to meet the organization's needs and support its activities, questions turn to the subject of how well the organization is anticipating the leader's desires and executing his plans.

More tellingly, the traditional employer/employee relationship is perverted. Having made so fateful a decision as to put so potent an individual in such a powerful position of leadership, the board of directors now finds itself bullied away from supervising and holding accountable the leader it hired. Rather, it is itself supervised and held accountable by the leader, and by internal and external observers as well, for how faithfully it fulfills the leader's desires and aids in the facilitation of his agenda. Far from exercising its fundamental role, protecting the interests of the owners, and supervising the activities of the leader, it becomes his confederate and intercessor with the shareholders. The board, often composed of a substantial fifth column of such leaders at the helm at other organizations, not to mention inside directors, abrogates its independence and responsibilities; it becomes complicit in the general surrender to the leader.

Thus, the one agency with the authority and ability to hold in check the burgeoning aura of leadership surrounding those at the head of today's organizations, and harnessing it to the needs and aspirations of the owners, fails to do so. Instead, it is, in its turn, routed by the runaway legend of the leader, neutered and rendered unable and unfit to do its duty. The new leader of today, swept into unprecedented power with the aid of the modern leadership movement, is left alone at the summit, constrained only by the vastness of the expectations placed upon him.

JUST ADD WATER

The other general grouping in the overall modern leadership movement shifts the emphasis to the members of the organization. It can, itself, be divided in two general approaches, one describing the leader's emancipating effects on the employees, and the other describing their emancipating effects on themselves. In both cases, an inordinate emphasis is placed on the remarkable personal transformations described or proposed by the various models, at the expense of the goals of the organization and of the rights of the owners.

At the Feet of the Master

A number of leadership gurus argue that leadership is open to all, and that we might be surprised to learn that apparently ordinary people in our midst are, in fact, leaders. These thinkers then go on to ascribe rather remarkable characteristics to these humble folk. Among these is the mission and ability to convert followers into leaders—even into "agents of change." Leaders scan the masses of followers, create mechanisms for the identification and selection of potential leaders among them, and, by the force of their leadership auras, develop them into apprentices who will learn to bear the torch in their turn, lighting the way for future generations. A brief review of some of the titles published by the leadership movement will unsurprisingly reveal that many of these characterizations, combining personal humility with evangelical charisma, are based on interviews, surveys, and analyses of leaders selected for review, based on one criterion or another, by various authors.

Yet, there is plenty of evidence that these leaders have long been encouraged to view their roles in this way. Since its very emergence, the modern leadership movement has reflected a strong desire to find a nobler role for our lives, in the otherwise dehumanizing industrial age, than merely to manage and be managed.

Since the days of the Hawthorne experiments, in which it was inadvertently discovered that employee productivity could be positively affected by the appearance of managerial concern for the employees' work environment, vitally important insights have been discovered regarding the way organizations really work. This work culminated in Douglas McGregor's development of Theories X and Y, which he used to explain the behavior of managers and employees in organizations. This will be reviewed again in the next chapter. It is sufficient, here, to note that Theory X purported to describe traditional managerial techniques built on the assumption that people do not normally like to work; they need to be coerced to engage in productive organizational activity. In Theory Y, McGregor proposed that work was in fact an important element of normal self-fulfillment; managerial regimes that incorporated this insight would result in greater productivity for all.

McGregor was beginning to shift the focus of study of organizational leadership away from the "great man" to the organization as a whole. Unfortunately, he passed away before he could complete a fully elaborated model of managerial leadership based on this theory. Just as unfortunately, less able successors have missed his fundamental insight regarding the true nature of leadership in an organization. The democratic branch of the modern leadership movement can be argued to have arisen from, or be heavily indebted to, McGregor's work. Nevertheless, they have focused on developing particular democratizing ideals, out of the context of the organization and its purposes. These commentators have returned the focus to the individual leader, as the font of enlightenment and betterment for the otherwise benighted employee.

This branch of the modern leadership literature is run through with talk about the need for the leader to value the employees, to listen to them, and to learn from them. For example, the theory known as transformational or mobilizing leadership starts from the promising notion that leadership should be widely distributed throughout an organization. It then, however, goes on to describe an environment in which leaders engage the hearts and minds of the employees, promoting an exhilarating upward spiral of mutually reinforcing morality and inspiration. This thinking doesn't merely wander from the core purpose of an organization, which is necessary to provide meaning to the activities of those in it: it strays (purposefully) into a patronizing solicitation for the betterment of what are viewed as otherwise helpless and morally underdeveloped employees.

Unfortunately, it did not end here. Leadership is all too frequently described by present day gurus as all about heart. It is intended for the transformation of people. It is evangelical and designed to inspire and enlighten. One author argues rather mystically that modern day leadership is about reviving in people their whole potential; it is about leading them back toward their own core selves.

The Leader Within

One of the ways this is done is by delegating leadership to the led. The principle vehicle for the development of leadership from the led is the use of teams. Teamwork has become an important element of the modern literature, and has taken up a value of its own, as has leadership itself, evidently free of the need for context.

Douglas McGregor used self-directed teams in his experiments with Theory Y. A short while later, the British business thinker John Adair developed the Action-Centered Leadership model, which placed great emphasis on the team. He argued that effective leadership consisted in the integration of the three spheres of the task, the team, and the individual. Like McGregor's theories, Professor Adair's ideas also represented an important assault on the notion of the individual as the great leader. However, they also were attacked as too simplistic by successors less able than him. These successors then proceeded to focus on the development of particulars of his ideas, while missing the more important and fundamental insight.

Adair stressed the preeminence of the task and the derivative importance of developing the team and individual in order to accomplish it. Nevertheless, the proponents of the modern leadership movement have focused on the team to excess. The subject has become a field of its own, with its own acknowledged father, Professor R. Meredith Belbin. It has a full complement of sub-fields ranging from developing task-specific teams, to international and intercultural teamwork. As in so many of the other subsets of the modern leadership movement, the subject has taken on an importance of its own, divorced of the meaning provided by context. As the field has matured, so has the hyperbole enfolding and promoting it. In fact, a prominent modern pair of leadership gurus describes the team as more than merely a gathering of superior intellects (so much for the average Joe), but, rather, as a "miracle."

The modern emphasis on teams as a vehicle for liberating the leadership within the employee is largely another misplaced effort to democratize leadership for its own sake. The team is overemphasized and employed out of context. It places excessive pressure on employees, who may be happy enough to find a way to contribute to the organization's goals, but are perplexed and wholly uninterested in having various of their inner personalities developed and exploited against their conscious will.

The two main groupings of the modern leadership movement vary from an overemphasis on the leader to an overemphasis on the led. The focus of the first group, on the exceptional qualities expected of the individual leader, is abusive of the position and exploitative of the occupant. Wholly untenable burdens and pressures are placed on this leader, which create an incredibly stressful environment. The various reactions resulting therefrom are presently a matter of unacceptably unfortunate public record and ongoing litigation. The second group places similarly unwarranted focus and pressure on individual employees and their leadership responsibilities, as expressed, in particular, in teams. The principle shortcoming of the overall movement is its failure to anchor discussion of the nature of an organization and its leadership in its purpose, which is to give expression to the aims of its owners. This, in turn, leads to a climate of uncertainty, unaccountability, and, ultimately, of moral jeopardy.

In the next chapter, we will discuss some early insights into the true nature of leadership in organizations. We will follow that, in Part II, with the development of the model of organizational leadership propounded in this book.

3

What's Close

Two problems with current models of leadership are the destructive identification of the organization with its leader, and the dis-identification of the leader with the organization. The organization and its fate are increasingly seen as deriving from the leader, but the leader sees himself as a distinct and independently operating entity. The democratizing branch of the modern leadership movement does little to mend the situation by its development of patronizing approaches to engagement with subordinate levels in the organization, or through an over-reliance on the presumed magic of teams.

Yet, there are hints in the literature as to what leadership really may be and how it may actually operate in an organization. Some of these have been developed by legitimately well-regarded thinkers in the management field. Nevertheless, their successors have, unfortunately, given little attention to such insights. The commentators have largely focused on the innovations visible in the more prominent and striking superstructures of these thinkers' ideas, stripping them of the context of the more fundamental conceptual bases on which they were intended to rest.

This chapter will examine those ideas in the literature that hint at the true role of leadership in the organization. In the development of this thinking, there has emerged a generalized sense that leadership can be viewed as a culture that permeates the organization, and that can be cultivated and modified to better serve it. This theme is, itself, a useful, though incomplete, advance. It will be addressed at the conclusion of the chapter. Presently, it is sufficient to review those thinkers who have contributed to the key insight that there are various degrees of value extant in the organization's personnel that it is management's duty to discover, develop, and harness. Many of these have specifically addressed the question of what leadership is, and the chapter will begin by reviewing their answers.

RELATIVE

Douglas McGregor was a pioneer in this endeavor. In 1960, he published his Theory X and Theory Y models of management. Theory X is based on the traditional managerial notion that people do not naturally enjoy work and must be coerced into productive performance. McGregor counterpoised Theory Y, based on the idea that work is a fundamental element of human self-fulfillment. Of particular reference to the discussion in this book, he argued that people are willing to exhibit self-generated initiative and commitment to organizational goals when properly encouraged and enabled to do so. He believed that management that acknowledges this and incorporates it into its management regime would in fact be more productive.

McGregor evidently enjoyed considerable success in applying Theory Y in a Proctor & Gamble installation, developing it into the most productive unit in the firm. On the other hand, however, Abraham Maslow, who was a strong supporter of Theory Y, was unable to match McGregor's success in application. On the contrary, he found it necessary to re-introduce into his management regime some directive features reminiscent of Theory X, in order to provide structure and focus to an organization that had begun to drift.

McGregor supported the introduction of innovations such as decisions by consensus, and organizational interest in the overall welfare—even in the social lives—of its employees. The key underlying insight that made sense of such innovations was McGregor's observation that leadership in an organization is too broad a topic to rest solely on the person of the leader. He believed that leadership incorporated a range of factors encompassing the whole organization, its members, and its environment, and that it could only be properly understood as the relationship among these variables. Unfortunately, this aspect of McGregor's thinking was largely ignored, while the specific ideas deriving from it were developed in generally non-viable directions, due to being uprooted from the context that caused them to make sense.

On the one hand, McGregor argued that leadership is not an individual characteristic, but is more properly viewed as the relationship between variables extant throughout the organization, including its structure, its operational policies, and its environment. This was an important assault on the (still current) belief of the uniqueness of the individual leader. On the other hand, however, he diluted this argument by further describing leadership as the relationship between the individual leader and the situation he faced, as formed by those organizational variables he identified. While McGregor's observations regarding the true nature of the work force and its motivation have had enduring positive effects on management thought, his insights hinting at the true nature of leadership failed to gather momentum.

STRUCTURAL

Some 18 years after McGregor published his theories, James MacGregor Burns launched another assault on the popular notion of leadership as residing in the individual. He argued that we knew too much about the character of leaders, and not enough about the phenomenon of leadership. He noted, tellingly, that the numerous discrete and separate definitions of leadership have fragmented and diluted the integrity of the idea itself.

Instead, Burns identified the concept of leadership as a structure that generates unity of action. Here, we have a definition that is built on the notion of goals, and the organizing of people to harness their efforts in the achievement thereof. Burns argued that leadership, viewed this way, permeates society at all levels and in numerous ways, engaging people, in varying degrees, in the collaborative pursuit of various purposes.

Burns saw the manipulation of this leadership structure as occurring in two basic manifestations. In his transactional leadership model, leaders and employees exchange tangible items of value in a manner designed to integrate individual and organizational needs and goals. This model is based on clearly communicated goals and detailed planning, conducted in the context of a formal structure that facilitates the identification and execution of the numerous reciprocal exchanges of value upon which the system depends.

The model suggests an environment in which people cautiously measure others' demands against their own needs, basing their collaborative endeavors on a calculated compromise of self-interest. In contrast to this, he also posited the idea of transformational leadership. In this model, instead of warily counterbalancing each other's needs, leaders and followers raise each other to ever-higher standards of effort, and even morality, while joined together in the pursuit of common purposes.

The transactional model points at the manner in which people organize their needs within a purposeful structure, enabling them to integrate the pursuit of individual and organizational goals—the transaction serving as the basis for enabling the collaborative accomplishment of a purpose. The transformational model, on the other hand, emphasizes the positive effects on the leaders and followers, as the latter's hearts and minds are engaged by the former—the organization serving as a vehicle for the ethical and moral transformation of all its members. This, unfortunately, places an undue focus on subsidiary and derivative social benefits of work in a collaborative environment, at the expense of the proper goals, the pursuit of which led to the creation of the organization. It places leaders in a paternalistic and manipulative relationship with followers, who are expected to feel valued and elevated by the attention received from their leaders. This attention presumably promotes greater levels of motivation, and higher ethical and moral standards than, we are left to believe, the followers would otherwise have.

While the environment of self-interested calculation suggested by the first model is hardly inspirational of soaring accomplishments, it at least has the value of placing due emphasis on an acknowledgment of the purpose of the organization's existence, and building thereon a structure for the collaborative accomplishment of its goals. This permits the sustenance of an environment in which individuals can continue to meet their goals, as well. Further, it does not preclude the introduction, on a derivative level, of certain features of the transformational model.

This lesson is second nature to many military organizations, as will be discussed further in future chapters. In connection with Burns's ideas, it is sufficient, here, to note that in the military, the first priority is accomplishment of the mission, and the second is looking after the welfare of the soldiers. The primary goal of a tasking in the military is its accomplishment, not to serve as a vehicle for the transformation of the soldier. To reverse these, however well meaning, is likely to result in endangering the accomplishment of the one as well as the welfare of the other. This is no less true in an economic or political sense in a non-military environment and organization.

The principle value of Burns's insights is twofold: 1) his identification of leadership as a phenomenon distinct from the leader, and 2) his description of leadership as a structure facilitating collaborative action. Unfortunately, the then unique ideas presented in his transformational leadership theory attracted the bulk of attention among management and leadership thinkers, and his more important and fundamental thinking on the nature of leadership were largely overlooked by his successors.

CIRCULAR

In the 1970s, the British organizational leadership guru John Adair promoted his theory of action-centered leadership. This is based on the idea that to be effective, leaders need to address three areas of activity related to the task, the team, and the individual. The basic idea is that a task calls into being a team or organization to pursue it, and this, of course, is composed of individuals. These three areas can be viewed as circles that overlap, indicating their interrelatedness. None can be viewed in isolation, and all must receive leadership attention in order for any to work effectively and for organizational goals to be met. Further, Professor Adair saw leadership as occurring at three levels: 1) that of the team, 2) the operational level where the activities of teams are designed and coordinated, and 3) the strategic level.

The advantage of this view is that it, like McGregor's, sees leadership as occurring in organizationally significant ways at levels other than the top. It points out that leadership attention must be directed toward the needs of humans and institutions within the organization other than itself. Further, like Burns, Adair makes a clear and distinct connection between leadership and action—the generation of activity directed toward the accomplishment of organizational goals.

Adair does a service by redirecting the dialogue on leadership from the individual leader to the organization, and to suggest a more comprehensive view of it than as merely an extension of the will of the individual leader at the top. Nevertheless, he does not go far enough in de-coupling leadership from the leader. In fact, he argues that leadership is a function of the individual leader, and has published several works designed to teach to individuals the secrets of leadership, and techniques for discharging it.

Just as unfortunately, Professor Adair's ideas have been criticized as too simplistic. That he expresses observations that others describe as only too obvious does not explain why those others have themselves either not made them, or have paid insufficient attention to them. It is hardly a praiseworthy feature of academic rigor to dismiss what is acknowledged as true because it appears to be too readily grasped by the common man. Furthermore, his critics construed his ideas as endorsing authoritarian and hierarchical structures that paid insufficient heed to the popular exhortative themes of the day. Modern organizations, these critics insisted, should be flexible, aggressively challenge the status quo, promote change, and empower and transform the employee. Once again, valuable insight on the fundamental purpose of leadership is lost in the din of tangential ideas divorced of their derivation from the core concepts and purposes that give them meaning.

SITUATIONAL

Another insightful writer on leadership and management was Kenneth Blanchard. In the late 1980s, he argued that leadership could be exhibited via four basic expressions: directing, delegating, coaching, and support. The key to his insight, however, is not in yet another delineation of models of leadership, most of which were meant to stand in negative contrast to the one the writer proposed as the only, or at least preferable, alternative. Blanchard took the view, novel to the business community, that each style is equally valid—even preferable—under suitable circumstances. The different styles were not arrayed along a continuum of organizational development and maturity, but related to varying situations in which any organization, at any age, could find itself.

Further, Blanchard reversed the traditional relationship between leaders and followers. In his view, the followers should not serve the leaders—rather, the reverse. The role of the leader is to serve the employee, and to ensure that the latter has the facilities, training, and support necessary to accomplish the task. Further, this service, provided by the current generation of leaders, develops the employees' capabilities to move up the organization over time, becoming the next generation of leaders and, thus, maintaining the organization's vitality and viability.

Professor Blanchard propounded a view of leadership that gave organizations a much more realistic and flexible means of dealing with the widely varying unfolding of circumstances in the real world. He presented it in a concise and persuasive fashion that brooked little quibbling. Further, he asserted that leaders served both the organization's goals and the employees charged with executing the tasks designed to accomplish them. This was also a direct and concise insight that, once expressed, was difficult to object to. As a result, many in the management and leadership thinking community were dismissive of his contributions, for the very reason that they were so obviously on the mark.

Fortunately, the business market was considerably more receptive of Professor Blanchard's writings, purchasing them in numbers that are multiples of what his critics were able to generate. Nevertheless, the more fundamental implications in Blanchard's ideas for the true nature of leadership were not picked up and developed by subsequent thinkers in the field. Another opportunity was lost to approach a more accurate model of leadership for the use of the organizational community.

Emotional

The subject of emotional intelligence is attracting growing attention in several fields, including, increasingly, management and leadership. Observers have noted that the traditional view of intelligence, as strictly the possession of knowledge and the ability to manipulate it, does not serve as a particularly effective predictor or promoter of success. Many people who are viewed as being intelligent by the traditional standards are not successful, and many who are not especially intelligent according to those standards are quite successful. Emotional intelligence is an attempt to capture a broader basket of capabilities that more effectively comprehends this phenomenon.

Proponents of the concept of emotional intelligence relate it to leadership in a manner reminiscent of Blanchard's insight that leadership's role is to serve the organization's employees. The argument is that a large proportion of business productivity arises from the organizational work environment, and a substantial portion of that is dependent on the abilities of the leader. Two conclusions are presented as following from this: 1) a leader's success is derived in large measure from his ability to create a work environment that facilitates employee and organizational productivity, and 2) in order to do this, the leader must learn emotional intelligence.

The observation that productivity arises from a work environment suggests a comprehensive view of the value of the employee to the organization's ability to effectively accomplish its goals. The observation that the development and maintenance of this work environment depends on the skills and abilities of the leader suggests that it is more than merely an enlightened aggregation of the latest transformational or enabling fads promoted by exhortative-style management and leadership thinkers. Rather, since it results in productivity and arises from the skill of the leader, it is a regime of managerial methods that has the effect of promoting activity that is efficiently directed at the production of results.

Thus, the overall effect of the application of emotional intelligence to leadership in an organizational environment potentially has two key benefits. One is the comprehensive view of the roles of leaders and employees in an organization and their mutual purpose for being in it. The other is the approach's built-in tendency to integrate technique with intent, offering the potential to spare it from the de-coupling of method and context suffered by other promising approaches.

Unfortunately, another difference between this and most of the other approaches mentioned in this chapter is that it does not address the fundamental nature of leadership as promisingly as they do. It offers useful ideas based on strong argumentation for the purpose of leadership, but it still places its execution in the individual leader. It then goes on to invest that leader with yet another distinctive ability tending to enhance his special status and uniqueness within the organization. The search of the literature, then, must continue for an effective and accurate appreciation of what leadership really is.

ORGANIZATIONAL

While the contributions above are insightful and point the way toward the proper understanding of leadership in organizations, they do not quite arrive there, themselves. Furthermore, it is disheartening to observe that subsequent writers on the topic have largely strayed from the fundamental to the tangential, which they further marginalize by denuding it of its context. It should not be surprising, then, to find that to approximate more closely the actual situation, we need to go further into the past.

In the late 19th and early 20th centuries, Mary Follett emerged as a brilliant practitioner, observer, and writer on the topic of organizations. Her most prolific writing on the subject was in the late 1910s to the early 1930s. During this time, businessmen in the United States and the United Kingdom frequently sought her views and advice, and she can be considered one of the first true management consultants.

Follett observed that individuals had a natural tendency to seek organization in groups. She went on to argue that groups possessed a natural internal dynamic that led to the consensual formulation of goals, and plans of action for attaining them. Adapting a sort of dialectic theory, she argued that disagreement leading to conflict was both a natural and, properly managed, positive group phenomenon that helped uncover the best directions and alternatives for the group. By this process, individuals identified their and others' interests, adapted them to each other, and developed group interests, associations, and activities. In the course of so doing, universal group problems of power and conflict arose. Who should have access to power? Who should wield it? How? How can conflict be controlled and used creatively?

Initially, Follett viewed these issues from a social perspective. Particularly after World War I, social observers, in general, reacted to the horrors of the war by recoiling from the sort of power arrangements that were believed to have caused it. Many of these writers proposed alternatives, some of which have been shown in the course of time to be unduly utopian. Follett, as well, delved into efforts to prescribe preventative solutions to such conflict gone awry, particularly in the years after the war. In the 1920s, however, she increasingly directed her thinking to issues confronted by organizations more generally, including business organizations. She was also among the pioneers in the application of the insights offered by psychology to the understanding and management of organizations.

In applying her thinking on the behavior and dynamics of groups to organizations generally, Follett concluded that their management is also a natural feature inherent to them. That is, it tended to, and was often best left to, occur naturally within the organization. Follett observed, for example, that workers in specific areas were often better informed regarding the nature of their specific duties than was management; thus, they were better left to determine how to organize and discharge those duties. Not only did the workers have a more intimate knowledge of the details of a particular task, but they also were better acquainted with how its performance might influence elements within and without the organization that were affected by that performance. A deliveryman, for example, not only knows best how to organize his route from an efficiency standpoint, but also from the standpoint of customer satisfaction.

As a result, Follett believed that effective management could not exist and emanate solely from the top of the organization. While she still ascribed inordinate value to the foresight and charismatic vision of the individual leader, she nevertheless succeeded in making a fundamentally important distinction between authority and leadership. Follett believed that the group naturally performs many of the functions of its own leadership and management, and that the senior administrator's principal duty is to monitor and efficiently coordinate this phenomenon to the benefit of the organization.

This is a profound insight. It is a breakthrough that represents a major advance toward a proper understanding of what organizational leadership is, how it operates, and how to manage it. Unfortunately, it did not meaningfully survive her. The attraction of various great man theories of leadership proved too powerful. She died in 1933, as events around the world were leading to the next world war. The next generation of observers of organizations was influenced by that war, and by the leaders who stood so large against its backdrop. Events appeared to be too vital and too urgent, and they clearly seemed to demand decisive and forceful individual leadership. As those influenced by the large and momentous enterprise of the war emerged, on its conclusion, to undertake the equally demanding endeavors called into being by its close, the models provided by the war were adapted to their new efforts. Follett's ideas were lost.

CULTURAL

In the first chapter, we observed the general tendency of management and leadership thinkers to remain tied to the influence of the view of leadership as residing in the individual. A democratizing tendency attempted to recast the debate, but succeed only in trivializing it. In the next chapter, we took a closer look at some of the more deleterious characteristics of the modern leadership movement's prescriptions, both in the concentration, and in the dilution, of the individual leadership model.

In the present chapter, we have reviewed attempts to break out of the unproductive model of the organization dependent in detail, inspiration, or both on the leadership at the top. We have seen insights that tend to arise from observations of how organizations—and the people in them—actually work.

This, in turn, has led to a general sense of leadership as a cultural feature of the organization. Proponents of organizational culture identify it directly with organizational leadership, and describe it as developing in a predictable and linear fashion from birth to maturity. This is a promising line of discussion, inasmuch as it contains the potential for generating a sophisticated and elegant model of leadership, reminiscent of Follett, which arises naturally from the organization, rather than from an individual. Unfortunately, just the opposite tack is taken. An organization's culture is described by the movement as being created, cultivated, and influenced by heroic top leaders. Thus, it is seen as an extension of their personalities, and of their individual leadership traits.

The senior executives at the top most decidedly influence the culture of an organization. However, it is a fundamental inaccuracy to identify leadership as something that is directly or indirectly imposed on, or insinuated into, an organization by its top leaders.

This book will argue that leadership is simply another natural feature or resource of an organization. It is neither particularly superior nor inferior to any of the others. Making it appear to be so trivializes both those who do so and the contribution that it is able to make to the organization. Leadership is an organizational asset to be managed like any other.

In order to develop this idea, the chapters of Part II will endeavor to describe what leadership really is, and how it operates in an organization. This will begin with a discussion of how the operation of leadership in an organization affects the organization. It will then describe the affects of the organization on its leadership. This particular discussion will lead to a reassessment of what leadership really means, and from where it arises. It will also complete the argument that leadership is not a culture in and of itself, associated with or applied to an organization, but is fundamentally an element of the broader organizational culture.

Next, the functions of leadership will be reviewed with particular reference to the argument developed in the preceding chapters. Attention will center on how to manage the organization's leadership resources in order to accomplish the leadership functions throughout the organization.

There will undoubtedly be vigorous resistance to many of the ideas presented in this book. Decades, even millennia, of historical experience and intellectual habit have accustomed us to view leadership as an individual characteristic exhibited for the good or ill of mankind. Part III will begin with a chapter outlining the most vigorous of these challenges to the thesis of this book, and will endeavor to answer them. It will then conclude with a summary and discussion of the import of the ideas presented in the book.

First, we will turn to observers in the civilian and military realms whose insights bear meaningfully on our discussion. We will begin with the effects of leaders and leadership on the organization.

PART II
Organizational leadership

As for the best leaders,
the people do not notice their existence.

The next best,
the people honor and praise.
The next, the people fear,
and the next, the people hate.

…

When the best leader's work is done
the people say,
"We did it ourselves!"

Lao-Tsu

4

Leadership from the Front

"Unless a man has that virtue,
he has no security for preserving any other"

—Samuel Johnson, on Courage

When discussing organizational leadership, the military is often cited because it possesses a rich history of clear and challenging examples for study. All the functions of leadership are plainly required of military leadership. Further, the abilities of military leaders are often visible in sharp detail against the background of the momentous events amongst which they deploy their skills. As a result, they provide a rich source of material for observation, analysis, and comparison.

A NOTE OF CAUTION

Part II, which presents the argument underlying the central thesis of this book, will draw heavily on inspiration from military examples. Nevertheless, it is only prudent to offer a general caution regarding the applicability of lessons derived from military leadership to non-military environments and organizations.

To begin with, as indicated in Part I, virtually all of the literature on leadership discusses it in the context of the individual leader. Certainly, there would seem to be a surfeit of examples of successful and unsuccessful individual leadership in the military field. Nevertheless, there are two basic problems with using them to derive lessons for leadership in non-military situations: 1) the military operates in an environment unlike that of any other organization in important and irreproducible ways, and 2) leadership, even in the military, isn't precisely about the individual leader—it's about his command. Why exactly this is so will be discussed in greater detail in the next two chapters; here we will provide a brief overview.

The Military Environment

Military organizations are designed to generate and deploy deadly force in furtherance of the goals of a larger group.[1] They fight for or defend freedom, economic interests, and other vital concerns. They help raise new political entities and raze old ones. They destroy an enemy's—or perhaps merely a competitor's—ability to impede or thwart interests deemed vital to the state or larger group.

Those in them serve to promote or defend the vital interests of a larger group, of which they are generally members, and with the interests of which they typically feel a personal bond, to some degree. Fighting in a global war against fascism or international terror generates emotion and dedication at a level unlikely to be replicated among the managers or employees of the typical commercial endeavor, however worthwhile an enterprise it may be.

Further, those in the military know that they are deployed in situations of duress. It is typically when diplomacy has broken down or been brushed aside, when enemy forces are attacking your ships in port or your civilians in the course of their daily pursuits, that the military issues forth from the barracks. When it does, it generally does so not in order to persuade or dissuade, but to kill. The military is an organization that generates, delivers, and applies deadly force in a manner specifically calculated to kill human beings who are in the service of the enemy. Any military activities that do not do this directly are intended to facilitate the doing of it.

The result is an environment characterized by a sense of intensely high purpose and momentous stakes. The importance of the duties discharged by the military—to serve greater state interests in circumstances of grave distress—is singular. The stakes incorporate individual and state survival. The intended purpose of the actions undertaken by the military in the discharge of those duties—to engage in and emerge profoundly victorious from mortal combat—is distinctly exceptional. This environment exists nowhere else. The form of individual behavior exhibited by leaders in this environment and the lessons to be drawn therefrom, likewise, are unlikely to be required, to exist, or to prove reproducible elsewhere.

Military Leadership

The lesson that organizational leadership—even in the military—is a characteristic of the organization, and not the individual, will be elaborated later in this and the next chapter. The caution being offered here concerns the presumed lessons to be drawn from observation of the behavior of commanders in the military environment, and the assumption that these lessons can be applied to leadership in non-military contexts.

Variously strewn among the many characteristics thrown about concerning the individual leader are terms such as integrity, morality, and honesty. The usefulness to an individual in any environment of possession of these characteristics can hardly be denied. Particularly in the military, it can be vital for a soldier[2] to know that he can rely on the fellow on his left or right. It is also important for him to be able to have confidence in the honor and integrity of the commander who may send him into danger or order him to kill.

In civilian enterprises, it can also be helpful—even important—for employees to trust each other and those in authority. It is useful to know that one is engaged in an enterprise that produces a service or product that is a genuine value to the consumer. Nevertheless, the intensity of the purpose and stakes of military endeavors raises the importance of these individual characteristics to a level that is quite simply inappropriate—if not plainly ludicrous—when applied to the typical non-military enterprise. The unique and pronounced importance of key leadership characteristics in the military such as honor, morality, and integrity derive directly and ineluctably from the unique and pronounced intensity of the military environment in which that leadership is expressed. It is no use to declaim pedantically on their fundamental centrality in the absence of the context that confers on them that peculiar importance. To do so is to trivialize leadership as it manifests itself in the military. Moreover, it only serves to make a mockery of he who presumes to present himself as a leader engaged in pursuits as momentous for a civilian organization, its members, and the greater society, as those charged to the military.

It may be argued that there are individuals who are in what are traditionally viewed as leadership positions, such as coaches, heads of religious communities, and other pursuits, that legitimately attract substantial emotional attachment and dedication. Nevertheless, the importance of the character of the heads of such enterprises to those influenced by them should be viewed as that of an example, or a model, that some would wish to emulate. This function, however valued, should be separated from their roles as the heads of organizations, which they help manage to meet their goals. Those goals, however noble and worthy, are not likely to be of comparable scope to those served by the military. What they ask of their staff, in terms of sacrifice demanded of them and the direct impact of action to be administered to others, cannot be compared to what is asked of the military.

For example, we expect the coach of a high school football team to possess a high degree of outstanding personal qualities. The reason for this, however, is that he will inevitably serve as a role model and example to our children of mature adult behavior in a competitive enterprise. It is not because we believe that those characteristics are vital to enabling the team to win football games against other high school teams, as much as we would like to see that happen.

Again, in the typical commercial enterprise in our society of whatever scale, we also expect the senior administrators to possess a superior degree of the personal characteristics discussed with reference to military leadership. In this case, however, it is principally because they are charged with fiduciary duties of fundamental importance to the work and private lives of a wide range of people, their communities, and their investments. This book will argue that it is not because these characteristics are vital to the successful management of their organizations—certainly not to the degree that this is the case in the military.

Military organizations and their reason for being are fundamentally different than civilian organizations in their basic nature and reason for being. As a result, the prominent importance of the presence of moral characteristics of the highest caliber in the interpersonal dynamics of the military is different as well. Accordingly, study of these is of limited value in the non-military world, and arguing for the central essentialness of these virtues in non-military leadership environments is generally out of place.

It should be noted, on the other hand, that modern commentators also recommend to the civilian leader personal characteristics of the military leader other than those revolving around morality and ethics. These typically surround areas such as intelligence, creativity, and boldness. Their presence in various degree and combination have been attributed to specific victories throughout history, and the presence of an undefinable critical mass of them is said to have existed in some of the world's greatest generals.

This book will argue, however, that they need not arise from the individual leader. Whatever their source, their presence, even in the military, is no more (or less) significant to victory on the battlefield than it is to success in the marketplace. Furthermore, for every battle that has been won by genius, there is one in which the genius of one side was defeated by the presence on the other of a greater will to win. For every campaign that has been designed with breathtaking foresight and executed with logistical brilliance, there is one such that has been undone by the greater fortitude and steadfastness of purpose of the other side. In fact, most military victories at bottom can be attributed to force of will, with the other capabilities assigned an essentially facilitative role.

This characteristic combines willpower and courage. As will be seen, all of the functions of leadership can be fulfilled by someone other than the leader—and often best are. However, the one vital personal characteristic the senior executive is uniquely suited by position to bring to the organization is willpower, and the courage to give it expression at every level in the organization. In the military, this is most properly viewed as command presence. In the civilian world, it is effective management.

This brief discussion has been presented with the specific intent neither to praise the roles played by individual military leaders, nor to belittle those filled by individual civilian leaders. The purpose has been to point out the fundamental differences between the two that make uncritical analysis of the one for application to the other, at the very least, inappropriate.

There is value, however, in examining the operation of the military organization as an entity, and as a framework for the interaction of individuals engaged in a collaborative enterprise. In this case, the intensity of the enterprise, and, thus, of their interactions, may indeed more clearly than otherwise reveal lessons of value. These lessons, validly drawn from the military for application in the non-military organizational environment, are not of individual, but of organizational leadership. It is to this endeavor that we will now turn.

MEN AGAINST FIRE

S. L. A. Marshall served on active duty with the U.S. Army in World War I, and as a combat historian in both the Pacific and European Theaters in World War II. In 1947, he published *Men Against Fire: The Problem of Battle Command*, which has become a classic study of the behavior of men in combat units.

Marhall's principal intent was to build on the striking data he reported, regarding ratios of fire employed in American combat units under fire, in order to draw attention to the need to revamp the way US soldiers were trained, at that time, for combat. Marshall made a variety of specific proposals for how to develop training programs, many of which proved to be important contributions.[3]

However, it is his body of observations about how soldiers and military units behave in combat that have survived the test of time. Marshall was an experienced and astute observer of the interaction of men in combat organizations, and of the effects of these interactions among them and on the organization as a whole. His observations about how men feel, think, and react in combat continue to strike a chord with those with operational experience in the military. They deserve an audience, as well, among those in the civilian world with a need to understand the reciprocating and reverberating effects of individual human behavior within and upon organizations operating under the stress of competitive conditions.

In particular, Marshall's observations about human interaction under conditions of uncertainty and stress suggest revealing insights regarding the real nature of organizational leadership—and of individual command. It is from one of these observations, in particular, that this and the next chapter will draw.

Action and Inaction

A fundamental element of American military doctrine for small unit offensive operations is the concept of fire and movement. This is, essentially, the performance by military individuals or small units of a combination of mutually reinforcing and alternating actions of firing upon and physically moving toward the enemy objective. In *Men Against Fire*, Marshall argues that, from the perspective of both the individual and the unit, rather than as conceptually distinct and separately performed acts, fire and movement are best conceived of as components of the same act. A man who is engaged in firing on the enemy is always looking for better positions from which to do so than the one he is currently in. These better positions are typically in front of him, closer to his target. As a result, he will move forward to the better position, fire, and then move forward again until he has attained the objective. He does not see the fire and movement that he is performing as separate activities. He simply performs them as a whole, intuitively integrating one as the part of the other. Marshall concluded from this that the soldier who will engage the enemy by firing his weapon will also move forward, advancing the unit's mission.

Conversely, the soldier who, for whatever reason, does not shoot will typically not initiate forward movement, either, lacking a compelling reason to do so. Thus, he may act as a brake on the forward momentum of the unit. On the other hand, Marshall repeatedly observed, in units containing both types of soldiers, that, when the shooter moves, the non-shooter moves up alongside him. In this case, while the non-shooter does not initiate action that advances the unit's accomplishment of its mission, neither does he impede it.

In fact, Marshall observed that the behavior of such soldiers in not firing their weapons does not reflect lack of courage or dedication. Ordinarily, these soldiers neither leave their posts nor shrink from danger. However, in the stress of combat and incoming fire, often but not exclusively for the first time, everyone has gone to cover and the soldier no longer sees or feels the presence of his fellows to his flanks. In fact, he typically does not see the enemy, either. The battle is joined on a battlefield that suddenly has become empty of both friend and foe. Alienated from his friends and disoriented at the presence of danger, the origin of which is difficult to determine, the soldier simply stops proactive efforts. He hunkers down and waits.

The shooter, on the other hand, does not naively fire and advance independently of what the rest of his unit is doing. He identifies the firing position ahead that offers an acceptable combination of advantages over his present position, and that is not too far forward of and isolated from the present line of his fellows. He then moves there and fires from it, generally without further movement.

Upon this, the non-shooter is disquieted by the sense that friendly soldiers have shifted forward. His instinct is to move up alongside of them, and, whether at their behest or on his own, he does so. He still may not fire. Now, it is the shooter's turn to be reassured that, while he has been firing, friendly soldiers have rejoined him on his left and right. He is once more in the midst of his own unit, and he turns his attention yet again to the search for a better position from which to support its mission, a forward position. The process begins again.

Marshall's concern revolved around what he believed to be the dangerously high ratio of non-shooters to shooters. The total amount of fire placed on the enemy is a major factor in bringing about his defeat. Marshall's intent was to draw attention to the situation, and to promote training methods that would mitigate it. In fact, he believed that improved training techniques did have a positive effect on the situation by the time of the Korean War.

However, in describing the persistent phenomenon of the two types of soldiers and their interaction in combat, he pointed to insights about organizational behavior and leadership that have important applications to the proper understanding of all organizations.[4] Of particular interest for the present discussion is the nature of the leadership performed by the minority of soldiers that Marshall described as shooters. He observed that they shouldered by themselves the responsibilities and risks of undertaking those tasks necessary to advance the unit's mission. These are the men who *did* something—they fired their weapons on the enemy positions, and sought out increasingly effective locations from which to do so. In the course of this, they moved the entire unit toward its objective.

SPONTANEOUS LEADERSHIP

All sorts of organizations generally have a number—typically a small minority—of proactive members who take the initiative to shoulder tasks important for all, or who seek out better ways of doing things, developing lessons from which all benefit. Often, this behavior is not specifically requested, is left unrewarded, and even goes unnoticed. It is the behavior of ordinary members, not from the top, but from within the organization. Where there is good guidance from above, this behavior amplifies and enacts it. Where there is not, it tends to emerge to fill the vacuum. It is worthwhile, then, to take a closer look at some of the ideas suggested by Marshall's model of individual active leadership—leadership that emerges from within the organization, pulling it forward toward accomplishment of its goals.

Follow Me!

Why do certain people take on risks and responsibilities, engaging in activity that combines proactivity with advancements toward accomplishment of their organizations' goals? In the military, it can easily be argued that this is done out of a concern for the group, its welfare, and its accomplishment of its mission. Presumably, all its soldiers feel that concern, but in the disorienting stress of combat, only a small number are able to act on it.

However, the general existence of this phenomenon would appear to argue against that, or at least to argue that there is an additional factor, or factors, at work. In the typical civilian organization, the stress encountered when the group engages in its chartered activity can be great, but it is not likely to approximate that felt by a soldier on the battlefield. A business unit entering a new market, a research team gathering and examining unexplored data, even a bureaucracy responding to a changing environment—all experience the phenomenon of a minority of their members taking the initiative. A small number will confront the issue, plunge in, take some action, and move the group forward. The others seem to passively await this behavior, and then acquiesce and accommodate themselves to it.

This behavior can arise out of a concern for the group, just as in the military. In the stress and disorientation caused by the challenges newly presented to the group, or for which it was newly created to address, some members, however eager or pleased they would be to personally contribute, can react to the new situation with uncertainty and tentativeness. In fact, their desire to contribute can add to the stress that clouds their ability to do so. Conversely, others' ability to puzzle out the problem can become more focused. Still others may not have any particularly clear impression of the problem or how to address it, but may conclude that the only way to develop this is to enter into the fray and see how things proceed, learning from that and adjusting as they go.

It can be extremely difficult to predict, in any group at any particular time, who these leaders will turn out to be, or where in the organization they will appear. The organization, of course, will have people in official leadership positions at various levels, but the individuals who actually take proactive action may be, and often are, an entirely different set of people. They may be Marshall's front line soldier, or Mary Follett's deliveryman. These may discover the real issue confronting the organization, the real means of addressing it, and they may be the ones who turn out to be proactive about doing so.

Most organizations have people who are widely recognized as "doers," or "go-to" individuals, who can generally be counted on to create ideas and generate constructive activity. Just as often, however, these proactive individuals can turn out to be leaders in one situation, and passive followers in the next one, which may result in the generation of a different set of equally unlikely leaders. Alternatively, there may be those who tend to more or less consistently display proactive behavior in one group of which they are members, but just as consistently not do so in another group.

It is inordinately difficult to determine who will display leadership activity, of what sort, and under what circumstances. It would appear, however, that the group, as Mary Follett argued, will generate people to fill these roles. In Marshall's model, it certainly was the case that the military units he observed had formal leaders. Nevertheless, however effective those leaders were, the units needed leadership activity of types and at levels where it was not or could not be provided by the formal leadership. A unit's officers or other formal commanders couldn't be at every location on the field of battle, and their absence from any part of it for any period of time could not be allowed to mean the absence, as well, of leadership. That leadership had a tendency to emerge where it was needed. It could be by the same individuals time after time, or different ones in different circumstances. It could be by soldiers who were unruly and uncontrollable in barracks, or by those who consistently showed discipline and soldierly virtues in all areas.

The same occurs in civilian organizations of all types, and it is just as difficult to predict where, how, or by whom it will be demonstrated. It may be that some of Marshall's soldiers, on a particular battlefield at a particular time, saw an opening that only they could use for the benefit or protection of the unit, so they used it. In civilian organizations, it may be the sales representative who is able to see the new market that the business unit needs to enter. It could be the research intern who comprehends the key to framing the research problem, or to interpreting the data. It might be the counter clerk, or the legislative liaison, who is able to alert the bureaucracy to changing circumstances. At different times, it might be the marketer or the engineer who becomes fired up about new possibilities, or the research data analyst who comprehends the issue, or the unit auditor who detects changing circumstances. It is difficult, probably impossible, to predict who will exhibit it on any given occasion. However, it would seem to be predictable that it will occur. Perhaps that is the key lesson for the manager. It is one to which we will return in Chapter 7.

I'll be Waiting Right Here

For now, let us consider Marshall's observation that the battlefield leaders tended to move a certain distance ahead of the present friendly lines in order to find better firing positions. The idea was that movement and fire were connected in a way that caused the shooter to instinctively sense that there was a shooting position a little further ahead that was better than the one he was presently in. Yet, after moving up from friendly lines, he did not continue independently moving forward into those superior positions. Why? Why did the proactive leader in Marshall's model lead so far, and no farther?

In the case of a soldier on the battlefield, moving too far ahead, beyond the support of the rest of the lines, would probably expose him to danger without contributing to the mission of the unit. However, he was exposing himself to danger as it was, and, as Marshall has explained, the rest of the soldiers in the lines often were not supporting him, anyway. They were simply a passive presence to his flanks, or when he had advanced, a short distance to his rear.

The answer is that these soldiers were not behaving out of self-interest, to highlight their abilities, advance their careers, earn medals, or to hone or burnish their reputations as individual leaders. The actions they expressed arose from their presence as members of the group under the peculiar circumstances it faced, and their peculiar positioning amidst those circumstances. Their actions were instinctive, automatic, or unconscious, but they were not simple expressions of individual proclivities. They were performed—instinctively, automatically, or unconsciously—with reference to the group.

Advancing forward a bit to improve their ability to bring fire on the enemy made an instinctive sense—but only in the context of the needs and interests of the unit. Continuing to advance without being joined by the group did not make sense, and it was not done. The shooter waited there until the members of the rest of the group behind him, disquieted and restless at sensing some of their number shifting forward away from them, moved up and repositioned themselves alongside him. He sensed their presence again and, reorienting himself to them as they did to him, he—or another who saw a better position and opportunity to attain it—advanced again.

The parallel here for the civilian organization is not specifically that those who proactively express needed leadership functions should do so only to a limited extent. That does tend to be the case. Leaders will make a proposal, take an action, and generate support. However, they will then wait to see that this has been accepted and incorporated, or adjusted to, by the rest of the staff. Only then will they, or others, build on it with further measures. The military soldier's comprehension of this lesson arises instinctively from his membership in the group. The dynamics of individual behavior in a civilian organization, with its less immediate and demanding levels of stress compared to the military, tend to result in relatively weaker degrees of group cohesion. Nevertheless, the civilian leader at any level, and in any circumstance, just like his military counterpart, typically senses, or at least learns to appreciate, the need to avoid getting too far ahead of the pack.

The more fundamental parallel from this lesson, however, arises from what it suggests about the relation of leadership to the phenomenon of group cohesion. Individual expressions of leadership within an organization are instinctively understood by those expressing them to have meaning only in the context of the organization and its response to them. Marshall's soldiers would neither advance in the absence of the organizational impulse to do so, nor would they advance too far ahead of the organization, depriving their leadership of any productive meaning.

Inasmuch as the leadership arises from the organization, the nature of its expression is bound up with that organization and its evolving experience. As the organization accommodates itself to each initiative by some of its members, they or others build on that accommodation and its relationship to external experience to generate new initiatives and actions. As in fire and movement, these are not separate acts, but interwoven aspects of the same act. The one does not occur in the absence of the other. Neither does the organization, or its members, perceive their initiatives and the resulting organizational accommodation to them as separate acts. They naturally and intuitively occur together and arise, the one from the other.

This all might suggest that individual leadership from the top has no place in the organization. Its occurrence there is an aberration and a disturbance to its natural and proper functioning. This is indeed an intriguing argument, one apparently supported by the thesis of this book, and one we will return to in Chapters 6 and 7.

In this chapter, it is enough to note the relationship between how and why leadership is expressed by individuals in the organization, the fact of its existence, and the effects of its presence on the other members. The leadership occurs, not merely because there is an environment from which it can spring, but because there is an environment that demands and generates it. Furthermore, the organization *exploits* its leadership—but that topic is for the next chapter.

5

Leadership from the Rear

o o o o o o o o o o o o o o o o o o o o o o o o o o o o o o o o
"…every man is worth just so much
as the things are worth
about which he busies himself."

—Marcus Aurelius

The phenomena of group cohesion and leadership can appear to exercise profound influences on each other. In the context of this discussion, however, that is actually a distortion that surfaces principally when leadership is imposed on the group from the outside or above, typically in the form of individual leadership. Actually, the phenomenon of group cohesion should more naturally and properly be seen as *inclusive* of its own leadership.

This leadership arises naturally from within the group, and expresses itself variously among the group's members. As we saw in the last chapter, this can be seen in the spontaneous expression of leadership by some of the members of the group when it is under stress. As explored so far, this might suggest simply that the phenomenon of group cohesion causes certain individuals to come to the rescue of the group when it is under duress, to leap into the breech. This coincides with Marshall's view of the remainder of the group's members as being rendered passive by the stress of circumstances, if not passive simply by nature.

However, we also have noted that this leadership tends to be expressed in increments, themselves interspersed with accommodations thereto by the group. This suggests that a more interactive dynamic may be taking place between those in the group who, at any given moment or under any particular circumstances, are passive, and those who are active.

Marshall points out in *Men Against Fire* that the passive soldiers in a unit often do not detract from its ability to generate forward motion. In fact, he says, they may even contribute to it. While not initiating activity themselves, by advancing in response to the leadership displayed by the more proactive soldiers, they provide a physical contribution to the forward momentum of the unit. Their presence and behavior even act, he argues, as a stimulant to those who display the conspicuous demonstrations of leadership. They add moral strength to the unit and its cohesion, and help the active soldiers to keep up their work.

DIRECTED LEADERSHIP

Perhaps the contribution is more than merely supportive. Perhaps the spontaneous expressions of leadership are exhibited not solely for the benefit of—but also at the direction of—the apparently more passive members of the group. Consider the following:

In the early 1980s, of friend of mine and I, while serving as junior officers in the U.S. Marine Corps, happened to see the citation for a Silver Star Medal[5] that had been awarded to our commanding officer, Colonel James L. Williams, for his actions while a captain in combat during the war in Vietnam. He was cited for personally leading the men of his rifle company in a charge against heavy enemy fire, culminating in the capture of the enemy objective. The citation conjured up images of a heroic style of leadership that had been thought to have passed away with the days of the bayonet charge and massed infantry formations. Warfare, by the 20th century, had become highly technical, and featured the employment of weapons systems of deadly accuracy, and of fighting that was conducted from dispersed formations. Certainly, Marine front line commanders are famous for fighting alongside their men, rather than from command posts located to the rear of their own units. Nevertheless, the image of a warrior leader followed by files of his men shouting and charging uphill in the teeth of such deadly enemy fire called up visions of epic battles from eras of warfare that had long since passed into myth. We pictured our commander standing like a giant amid the enemy bullets and shrapnel, rallying his men with a heroic speech, bringing them to a pitch of combat ferocity that boiled over into an irresistible wave of valor, camaraderie, and dedication against which no enemy could stand.

"Well," he said with his characteristic humility, "it wasn't exactly like that."

He and the commander of the rifle company next to his were tasked with taking the objective. The enemy, however, managed to attain fire superiority, and poured rifle and artillery fire into the two Marine companies, pinning them down. Captain Williams moved to the point where his company linked up with the one to his side and discussed the situation with his fellow company commander. They intently sought to conjure up a way to break the deadlock, get their men out from under the enemy fire, and restore the momentum of the attack.

Colonel Williams explained that, as he and his buddy tried to puzzle out a solution, he happened to glance at his driver/bodyguard.[6] "Sir," the Marine said simply, "we're ready when you are." The two company commanders looked at the Marine, then at each other. The decision had been made for them. Their Marines were ready. When the commanders were ready, the attack would recommence. It was that simple. It also, the commanders sheepishly acknowledged, represented a tasking that had rather straightforwardly and unequivocally been presented to them for execution. They looked at each other again. They had been told that everyone understood what their duty was. They had also been told how to do it, and that it was clearly time to do it now. They each stood, turned to their Marines, and shouted, "Follow me!" A few minutes later, the objective was theirs.

These officers did what was necessary to take the objective and reclaim what was becoming an untenable situation for their units and men. They seized the moment, heedless of the danger. The commander of the flank company had a machine gun, which he used while leading his company's part of the assault. Colonel Williams, in telling us the story, neglected to add that he had passed into unit legend by brandishing aloft the only weapon at hand that he felt would be visible to his men and threatening to the enemy—a shovel. In fact, he and his fellow commanding officer also passed into Marine Corps legend and were known, along with a select few others, as the "Gunfighters" of Vietnam.[7] The courage under fire of these officers cannot be denied.

However, what was striking about Colonel Williams's story was what it said about leadership within the unit at that particular moment, while it was pinned down by enemy fire. Certainly, he was its commander, and, just as certainly, he was in command. He had the respect and obedience of his men. Further, he unquestionably displayed breathtaking valor and an unimpeachable personal example for his Marines by leading them in their charge to the objective. Under the stress of combat in the front line, when the situation demanded an instance of individual initiative—of leadership—in order to stimulate the group to action and advance it toward its objective, he personally provided that leadership.

However, as he said with the same simple and straightforward frankness displayed by his driver years earlier, "it wasn't exactly like that." That particular display of leadership, in that particular form, had come at the *direction* of the men:

"Sir, we're ready when you are."[8] Translation: "You can put the maps down. In the present circumstances, our best bet to regain fire superiority and the momentum is simply to rise up now and seize it by sheer unit will power and force. Lead us; we'll follow." The heroism and instance of personal leadership displayed by then Captain Williams on that day had been a part of a whole; an inherently interwoven element of the esprit and leadership of his unit. His advance that day, and their following him, were not separate acts or events any more than is fire and movement—they were part and parcel of a unitary expression of organizational leadership exhibited by, and from within, the group.

NATURAL LEADERSHIP

Mary Follett taught that the group would naturally tend to generate its own leadership and develop its own management regimes according to its purpose, its environment, and its needs. She argued that the role of senior executives is to observe and coordinate these expressions of self-leadership and management, and keep them pointed toward the organization's goal. She thus made a profound distinction between leadership and authority.

Leadership arises naturally from within an organization. Stimulated by the existing nature and degree of group cohesion, and the stress acting on the group from the environment, it will naturally and proactively organize itself to understand and deal with the challenges it faces. Individuals within the group will detect the unique challenges or opportunities confronting the organization. They will then either themselves initiate group action on them, or communicate them to others who will see their import and how best to organize the resources of the group to deal with them. These others will, in their turn, generate instances of spontaneous leadership to address them. This is a generally positive phenomenon that can, nevertheless, lead to some distress if not guided and coordinated.

The Senior Executive

Some might suggest that the coordination is provided by managers, and the guidance by the modern leader, whether a transactional leader, an edgewalker, or anything in between. This, however, is merely to acknowledge the quite ordinary occurrence of the imposition of leadership on the organization from above. More to the point, the senior executives, who after all are part of the organization, may be expected to have the instincts to contribute instances of leadership, just as do many of its other members. The problem, however, arises from our having lost track of Follett's line of thinking, and from our failure to develop it.

Because of the events of the inter-war years, of World War II and the huge economic enterprises that followed it, leadership theory grew to center around the individual. The individual was seen as either the sole font of, or at least as the singular inspiration for, all the leadership expressed within an organization.

The spontaneous fulfillment of an organization's leadership functions from within has been either entirely overlooked or even suppressed, albeit often inadvertently. An organization's members will tend to yield to forceful leadership, whether spontaneously generated from among them, or consciously imposed from above. Particularly when it comes from above, this group response will be exhibited with a range of emotions from enthusiasm to resentment. Even when it is quite clear that the general guidance or specific prescriptions of this imposed leadership are wrong, out of touch, or otherwise harmful, the combination of leadership and authority will normally prove to be irresistible. Unfortunately, in such circumstances, the apparent unresponsiveness of the imposed leadership regime to input from within the organization often leads to bitterness, cynicism, and passivity of the sort that is decidedly nonstimulative to, and nonsupportive of, that leadership. Adaptation slows. The unit does not willingly accommodate itself to the imposed initiatives, but must be enticed or coerced to do so. It becomes an unwilling brake on the momentum behind initiatives of which it does not approve, rather than a silent but powerful force supporting, and even stimulating, that momentum.

This combination of assumption of control over expression of the organization's leadership functions, and of authority over the organization, is often confounded into the same thing. However, unlike fire and movement, or the organization and its leadership as propounded in this book, leadership and authority are not two sides of the same coin. As Follett observed, they are distinctly separate characteristics of the organization. While one can lead, or appear to lead, to the other, their interrelation is not necessarily inevitable or inextricable. In fact, the interrelationship of leadership and authority is best viewed as a delicate and transitory phenomenon—particularly in reference to the senior administration of an organization—one that requires careful and conscious management.

The principal contribution of the senior administration is, properly, twofold. First is to communicate the organization's goals. This does not necessarily mean to decide on those goals. That is usually best left to those with true responsibility to the owners of the organization's purpose, which is usually the board of directors. Thus, the senior executives do not develop a vision of the organization—they are best told what it is. Circumstances will often arise calling for them to recommend a new or modified organizational vision, or purpose, to the board. In such a situation, they still should not do so in isolation, but should draw it from the organization and its interaction from the environment; this will be discussed further in the next two chapters. Having developed a range of proposals, they should be presented to the board for selection and approval. Again, through this means, the senior administration is told what the vision is, and its primary role in the organization, with respect to that vision or goal, is to ensure its accurate and consistent communication in and throughout the organization.

In an organization characterized by the spontaneous expression of leadership from within, the consistent communication of the organization's goal provides a base upon which that leadership can form itself. It helps to develop identity. It describes purpose and the organization's relationship to the environment. It gives meaning to their individual roles within the organization. Thus, it provides the key impulse to the generation of group identity and cohesion. This is the mass, generating the gravitational force that unifies the individuals as a group, and that forms the basis of their instincts to act individually in the interests of the group. The group dynamics that Follett described begin here. At this point, the group's individuals begin forming their organizational identities and actions around these goals. They develop a group lens for viewing the environment in which their organization interacts, and for sensing and evaluating the threats and opportunities that it faces. They consider their individual contributions based on what they see from where they are in the organization. The possibilities for spontaneously generated self-management and instances of organizational leadership appear.

The senior administration's second role is to coordinate these efforts of the organization's individuals in pursuit of its goal. This is a large topic, ranging from training, through organizational design, to management of operations; it will be addressed in greater detail in the next two chapters. In an organization that is making use of its natural instinct and tendency to manage its own efforts to attain its goals, and to provide expressions of the leadership functions necessary to do so, an important function of the senior administration is to facilitate and focus that organizational phenomenon.

Authority and Responsibility

Mary Follett showed us that leadership and authority are distinct features in an organization. There is a tendency, however, to confound the meanings of terms such as authority and responsibility, both generally and with respect to each other. For the sake of the clarity of the subsequent discussion in this and the following chapters, this will require some elaboration.

There is a common saying that you can delegate authority, but you cannot delegate responsibility.[9] While you can direct a junior to discharge certain of your duties, and you can assign to him from your pool of authority to do so, it is incumbent on you to remember that it will remain you—not him—who is responsible to the board for the results.

The basic lesson is about supervision. The saying is not intended to inhibit delegation out of fear that a junior's actions will expose the senior to the condemnation of the board. Nor is it intended to imply that delegated authority must be micromanaged. On the contrary, the authority must be freely given. However, it must be monitored and supervised. The senior executive must learn to balance confidence in his juniors with his responsibility to the board. It was he who was hired by the board, and it is he—not his staff—that should expect to be held accountable by the board for the performance of the organization.

The senior executive who remembers this lesson will consider his delegations and the capabilities of his staff carefully. He will balance organizational priorities such as staff development with the gravity and urgency of events facing the organization. These are important and fundamental lessons, with much to teach about the nature of delegation and supervision.

It is the core of the lesson, however, that is often missed, and that is key to the present discussion. It is that, of the two resources given the senior executive by the board, authority and responsibility, only authority can be delegated.

Responsibility is viewed here as a resource for the executive, because it forms the basis for his moral and legal right to exercise the specified authority given him by the board to help him discharge the duties it has assigned him. From the board's perspective, the authority is divisible. The executive can pass it along to others as appropriate or necessary, as long as it is exercised to further the legitimate purposes of the organization.

His responsibility for the exercise of that authority, however, does not accompany the division and delegation of the authority. His responsibility is the source of the authority he exercises or causes to be exercised by others. From the perspective of the board, that responsibility remains wholly and always with the senior executive. All of his actions as senior executive arise from the responsibility with which he has been charged for the operation of the organization. Whatever he does, and however he does it, his authority to do so arises from his responsibility for the organization. He can assume all the leadership functions or delegate them. However, under no circumstances can he delegate his responsibility for the organization. The board should not look kindly on a senior executive who does not understand this, and who blames juniors for an organization's missteps.

The type of authority being described here is not the sort that arises from an individual's exceptional behavior, or from the admiration in which others may hold him. It is simply the ultimate organizational authority contractually vested in the senior executive by the board. It is, however, a plastic term. It describes a divisible source of legitimacy that can be hoarded, delegated, reclaimed, and redistributed at the will of the senior executive. It exists, however, solely to enable him to discharge the duties assigned him by the board, for which duties he alone is responsible. From the perspective of the board, that responsibility cannot be divided or delegated. The senior executive can hold others in his staff responsible to him for specific tasks, but that can only be a transient function of a specific delegated authority, and is properly no concern of the board. While the board may applaud or condemn specific delegations of authority, it is outside its fiduciary duty to even acknowledge delegation by the senior executive of any responsibility in any form. Any such transient delegations of responsibility are merely personal and discrete extensions of a rationale used to form the foundation for his delegation of authority. Fundamentally, his responsibility is permanent and indivisible, and all of it, always, remains with him.

Leadership and Command

Thus, the two fundamental characteristics of the senior executive, assigned him by the board, are his indivisible responsibility and his divisible authority. In the military, an officer who has been given these is said to have been placed in *command* of an organization, over which he exercises *command authority*.

The *authority* exercised in the organization, whether expressed by the commander personally or by a delegatee, derives from the commander, due to his indivisible personal *responsibility* for the performance of the unit. It is this authority—*command authority*—that Mary Follett distinguishes from the expression of leadership in an organization.

The legitimate authority, then, to direct the activities of an organization can only arise from the senior executive. This authority derives from technical, legal, and moral—that is, fiduciary—responsibility, and is to be distinguished from the sort of transitory and varying forms of non-official authority that derive from instances of the expression of leadership. That latter authority is actually more properly understood as moral legitimacy, or influence, arising from the confidence and trust placed in the non-official leader at the moment of, or during the exhibition of, the expressed leadership. It is distinct from, and need not be confounded with, command authority. Rather, the intelligent commander encourages, cultivates, and manages such leadership.

Consequently, a senior executive who has been given command of an organization need not see himself as obliged to personally discharge all the managerial or leadership functions of that organization. His fiduciary responsibility is to place his authority where it can promote and bring about their proper functioning in pursuit of the organization's goals. His role, in other words, is to manage the delegation and expression—not of his individual leadership—but of his authority.

He would be well advised, in fact, to be careful to avoid confounding the two. He should heed Mary Follett's admonition that the role of organizational authority in the exercise and expression of organizational leadership should not be overemphasized. Leadership is a natural phenomenon in the organization. His principal duty is to manage the application of his authority in ways that will focus, facilitate, and coordinate the expression of his organization's leadership.

Exploiting Leadership

Mary Follett described organizations as exhibiting conflict and dissent that had the potential to operate on the organization in positive ways, resulting in its better organization and evolution to meet new and changing circumstances. An organization that exhibits leadership from within is likely to generate such constructive debate about the organization, its management and leadership, its role in its external environment, and its success in fulfilling that role. In the course of this discussion, various individuals, at every level of the organization, will often be prompted by others to perform this duty for the organization, or to make that proposal to higher management. Whether on the shop floor or the sales route, whether in marketing or product/service development, individuals will take the lead in discovering what their unit, or the organization as a whole, ought to be doing, or how it ought to be doing it. As the resulting information is conveyed throughout the organization, others will see the import of the discoveries and find themselves impelled to act or to generate action on them. All the while, all the organization's members will be participating in the leadership process, whether actively or inactively. Whoever may be on the spot at any given moment, working out a new idea or a way to use it, he will periodically turn to see the others waiting their turn to move forward to the new positions he claims in the name of the organization: "We're ready when you are."

It is immaterial whether it is senior management or those on the front line who are managing to discover new and better products or services, or ways to interact with customers. In any case, those exhibiting this leadership should feel the pressure of the group as a whole straining to move forward—to, at any given moment, be shown the way by whoever, at that moment, is best positioned to see it.

Senior management's fundamental role, however, is to facilitate, observe, and communicate these instances of leadership within the organization—as well as their results—to all its units and members, and to direct its authority to those instances where it can best be used to the advantage of the organization. Their role is not to impose leadership from above, but to manage and give command focus to its expression from within the organization.

6

Leadership from Within

o o o o o o o o o o o o o o o o o o o o o o o o o o o o o o o o o o

"I have always thought the actions of men
the best interpreters of their thoughts."

—*John Locke*

Leadership from within the organization is a perfectly natural and ordinary occurrence. It has been remarked upon for centuries, but has not achieved the critical attention it deserves. Students of leadership have continued, or been encouraged by events, to focus on the phenomenon of individual leadership from above.

This focus has had generally unfortunate consequences. Principal among them is its inadequacy in properly explaining the spontaneous occurrence of unofficial leadership within organizations, sometimes referred to as the informal structure, or influence structure, of the organization. This phenomenon, while frequently observed, has gone largely unremarked. The critics and experts of leadership tend to bring all possibilities for greatness, and all faults for failure, back to the individual at the top. Furthermore, they encourage the individual at the top to see himself (or herself) as the leader, solely responsible for exhibiting all the leadership functions. Any exhibition of them by others is often viewed as a threat to the leadership of the senior executive, rather than as a valuable contribution to the organization.

In *Men Against Fire*, S. L. A. Marshall highlighted this phenomenon with the story of a unit that, during a difficult assault, had progressed victoriously to its objective largely due to the heroic foresight, actions, and example of a single sergeant. Everyone in the unit, including its commander, attributed the unit's success under challenging circumstances to the sergeant's leadership. Nevertheless, the commander was actually surprised at being asked why he had not recommended the man for a commendation. In his view, the sergeant had practically wrested control of the unit from the hapless officer. The fact that the sergeant had displayed leadership that was instinctively recognized and acknowledged by the men, and that was even largely responsible for the unit's victory, represented disloyalty and an unwarranted threat to the leadership prerogatives that the unit's senior officer saw as reserved solely for him.

Marshall's observations during the war led him to believe that this was an all-too-common attitude. He argued that command authority should be viewed, not as a right, but as a "responsibility to be shared" by all those in the organization who, in any given circumstance, are in a position—and who are often eager—to do so.[10]

Further, Marshall's observations and interviews made it clear to him that examples of spontaneous individual leadership from within a unit were often not fully understood by its commander. He asserted that there were numerous engagements ending in victory largely due to the heroism and leadership of individual soldiers, and that, in these situations, the unit commanders weren't always aware of the pivotal contributions of these, their own men.

These examples are not—and concerns regarding them should not be—limited to the military. Far from it. Civilian enterprises abound with examples of individual initiative, undertaken often at personal financial or moral risk—or at least absent any particular inducement or prospect for personal gain—which result in benefits for the organization, and which efforts either simply go unnoticed or are punished for threatening the administrative structure of the organization.[11]

The real role of managers is to manage—not suppress—these instances of leadership from within the organization. They should facilitate, develop, direct, and coordinate them. They should not shut them off and arrogate the role of exhibiting them in the name of the organization solely to themselves.

Nevertheless, they often do precisely that. Even when they do not specifically do so, they all too frequently do not understand the phenomenon of organizational leadership, and they mis-appreciate and mismanage it. The focus by post-World War II critics and observers on individual leadership has led to the apparent development of considerable knowledge and expertise in, as well as to prominent individual practitioners of what is, essentially, an irrelevant, if not destructive, form of leadership in the setting of organizations.

MISMANAGEMENT

A principle concern of this book has been over the mistaken emphasis of the modern leadership movement on the analysis and development of individual leadership. This has resulted in a tendency to invest the hopes and fates of whole organizations in the persons of individuals of presumed singular leadership ability. Some individuals, for some of the time, have indeed been able to successfully pull off the arrogation to themselves of the leadership functions of an organization. More often than not, however, their plans and efforts turn out to have been failures right from the beginning. On those occasions when their plans do work out, these leaders mistakenly attribute these initial successes to their own enduring personal representation of the leadership personality. This conclusion then encourages them to plunge the organization further ahead into eventual disaster.

Individual leadership as described by the modern leadership movement often leads, in fact, to relentlessly growing trends toward misdirection and mismanagement of an organization. Lack of success is attributed not to a failure of the leader to accord with reality, but to a failure of the organization to accord with the will of the leader. The visionary power of these leaders is advertised as able, and expected, to surmount and shape reality—but not to yield to it.

Positive thinking is a fine thing, and it can have beneficial effects on the perceptions and behaviors of both individuals and organizations. Nevertheless, it will inevitably lead to disappointment if it is not formed around a cognitive process that is, itself, based in a profound assessment and appreciation of reality. Positive thinking does not change present reality. It changes our understanding of its meaning, and the range of our possible actions in its context. This leads to behavior that can be used proactively to change future reality. This is far too complex and important an organizational effort to be left to an individual. When it is left, as at the prescription of the modern leadership movement it so often is, to the individual leader at the top, it generally results in mismanagement.

Still, the model of organizational leadership propounded in this book is no panacea, either, for an organization's ills. If its existence or operation in the organization is not recognized, as Marshall pointed out is so often the case, or if it is improperly managed, the result can be organizational disaster, as well.

I have suggested that many of the functions of an organization's leadership are spontaneously generated within it, and find expression naturally through its members. Mary Follett also proposed ideas similar to this in her writings about the social dynamics of groups and organizations. This is an important fact not merely for managers to acknowledge, but also to study and understand. All too often, it is dismissed in the literature with a reference to the existence of individuals in the organization who exercise some form of influence over the other employees. The typical prescription is that such individuals should be identified and, not to put to fine a point on it, co-opted.

This is an unfortunate and shortsighted approach. The actual character of the naturally occurring phenomenon of leadership within an organization is much more fluid than this approach suggests. It is also more resilient, observant, and valuable. As I have argued, it is a resource present within the organization that must be managed like any other. It is not, however, inevitably in step with the desires or needs of the owners of the organization. Unaddressed, it can take a number of forms that are inconsistent with the purpose of the organization and intent of its owners.

Free Spirits

Up until the 19th century, naval warfare was conducted with wooden sailing ships. When the time for battle approached, a warship's cannons were rolled into their firing positions and secured to firing ports for action. If a loaded cannon escaped from the gun crew's control, it would roll around the deck according to the pitch and yaw of the ship's motion on the water. It had become a loose cannon. It could go off at any time, and who knew where it might be pointing when it did?

In any organization, a key duty of management, like the gun crew of a ship, is to arm its employees with the skills and knowledge necessary to the task, and to deploy them in a manner disciplined by the organization's mission and circumstances. They should be aware, as well, that there is a natural tendency for managerial vacuums to be filled. If employees or units are undermanaged for any reason, individuals will tend to fill the managerial void, including its leadership subcomponents. The result could be a unit that has slipped out of the control of management, and has become like a loose cannon, careening around the organizational deck, primed to produce unexpected events at unpredictable moments.

It is difficult enough to guide an organization in today's choppy and uncertain seas. Managers who are unaware that groups will incline to generate their own leadership may find themselves contending, as well, with the appearance of unexpected behaviors in inadequately controlled units or groups of employees. Managers should be aware that undermanaged leadership might lead to loose cannons. Such units are not necessarily aware that they are a distraction, or even a danger, to the organization. They may not even realize there is anything unusual at all about their situation within the organization. However, the value of a unit's contribution to the organizational mission is assessed according to the direction it is facing when it "goes off." The thesis of this book is that leadership, as an inherent characteristic of the organization and its subunits, is a potentially valuable asset—but only actually valuable when it is properly acknowledged and managed.

Rebels with (or without) a Cause

Generally, the basic value of units that react to the absence or insufficiency of managerial attention may be essentially neutral. They may simply be attempting to fill a managerial vacuum and be wholly unaware of anything unusual or problematic about that. The contribution or detraction of such units from the organizational mission in such cases will largely be a circumstantial function that derives from coincidence, rather than from managerial action or inaction. There are cases, however, where units have not merely been neglected by management, but, rather, have actively slipped the managerial leash.

Any one of a number of events in the life of an organization, or even of one of its employees, can lead to a sense of misdirection or betrayal. An individual can generalize onto his work environment a particular problem he is experiencing in his private life. Depending on his abilities and positioning within the organization, this sort of rotten apple can warp the expression of leadership in his vicinity in the organization, disrupting normal productivity and injecting a sense of dissatisfaction and low morale into the organization.

On the other hand, such commonplace organizational experiences as a sense that a unit's employees are consistently overlooked for recognition or promotion, the imposition of an unpopular or improperly introduced policy change or organizational redirection, or an ineptly handled merger or acquisition, can cause the normally occurring leadership manifestation in a unit to be consciously directed against the expressed wishes of the larger organization. Such organizational rebellions are more common than generally acknowledged in the wider business literature. Consequently, when an executive eventually encounters them, he is armed with little in the way of theoretical or practical tools with which to understand and deal with the insurgency. Typically, it is simply crushed. There is a certain chilling effectiveness in such an approach for the problem at hand. It ignores, however, both the managerial shortcomings that allowed the insurgency to appear, and the very existence of the phenomenon of organizational leadership which was the vehicle for its surfacing. This leadership phenomenon is a permanent feature of the organization and its units. It is not crushed with any particular insurgency. It may become tamed, or it may become bitter in attitude, and express its discontent in more subtle and maliciously efficient forms. The effective manager will recognize its existence, analyze the inputs that lead to its manifestation in particular ways, and use what is learned to manage it more appropriately to the benefit of all.

Lost Souls

As observed previously, Marshall described the inactive nonshooting soldier as, nevertheless, a generally positive influence on the forward momentum of the unit. The presence of such soldiers emboldens the shooters to take action and move up, whereupon the nonshooters join them, and the same, or new, leaders then begin the process again. Every soldier visible to another on the line, whether active or passive, adds moral strength to the will of all. The overall effect is salutary, and an encouragement and inducement to positive and constructive manifestations of leadership by those in a position to do so. Yet, there is another possibility. The otherwise passive soldier, who can be described as stoically supportive in the advance, can, under certain circumstances, become actively uncertain or fearful of an engagement's outcome. He can lose his confidence and give ground. In such an event, loss of resolve radiates along the line. It begins to break, and a general retreat, or rout, ensues. Sometimes, unit commanders are unaware that this is happening until it is over, or are unable, notwithstanding the most drastic efforts, to rally the unit.

While instances of high turnover or drops in productivity in a civilian organization are typically assumed to be the result of an inhospitable work environment or dysfunctional pay or personnel policies, they are just as often a result of a loss of morale among employees in the operating units. Negative interactions from customers, vendors, or the organizational environment in general, are identified by the front line employees first. Outdated manufacturing methods, unfounded planning assumptions, or unexpected levels and expressions of rivals' competitiveness are initially felt by those front line employees. If there does not appear to be managerial awareness and acknowledgment of these concerns, a sense of futility can spread in the organizational ranks, converting the basic core of stoic supporters of positive leadership into sources of front-line organizational uncertainty and loss of resolve. Instead of the phenomenon of individual initiative and enterprise, the organization experiences employee turnover and loss of productivity. Management is often unaware of the problem until it is well advanced. By then, the source of the issue may be difficult to discern, or confidence in management may be so degraded that the progress of the problem is difficult or impossible to reverse.

Leadership as it naturally occurs within an organization can be a spontaneously constructive—or an irrelevant, distracting or destructive—influence on the mission of the organization. It is the responsibility of the manager to accomplish that mission, and to employ all available assets in order to do so. Management that is unaware of the presence of leadership as an inherent organizational phenomenon will not only fail to make the most advantageous use of it, but will likely unknowingly suffer from its expression in ways that expend organizational energy unproductively, or that more directly frustrate management efforts.

MANAGEMENT

The status of the field of professional management has suffered from considerable abasement since the rise of the modern leadership movement. In fact, it is increasingly common to find works on the business of running organizations that have extensive index entries for "leadership," but no longer have any about "management," at all. Nevertheless, overarching claims for the role of individual leadership notwithstanding, the traditional definition of management is the development of organizational objectives and the identification and deployment of resources to accomplish them.

This is pretty much the heart of it. The issue is to determine what needs to be done, what assets can be marshaled to do it, and how best to use them. All study, experimentation, and research on the topic are efforts to better understand and address these fundamental concerns. Whether the discussion is about labor or capital, decision-making techniques or issues of strategy and tactics, product development or marketing, human resource management or process management, at a basic level, it is about how to address one or another of the fundamental managerial concerns.

In truth, the same is true of discussions of leadership. While the case made in the first chapter will not be repeated here, it is appropriate to note, at this point in the argument of this book, that all the definitions of leadership are essentially aimed, as well, at one or another of these basic managerial issues. It will not do, then, to deny that the field of leadership was pilfered from that of management. Nevertheless, a new sort of professional was conceived—the leader—and his place was set above that of the manager. We learned that the leader was presumed to possess creativity, vision, integrity, force of will, and the ability to inspire followership. In other words, we heard a good deal about the individual qualities and responsibilities of the leader. We were never presented, however, with a generally accepted definition of the leader's area of professionalism—leadership—and what sets it above, not to mention apart from, management.

In fact, the descriptions of the leader, on closer examination, can be seen to be little more than hyperbolic extensions of the duties of the manager. While we may not, as a rule, associate words like "creativity" or "vision" with the idea of a manager, the possession of these characteristics does not necessarily convert the manager into something else. In fact, it is entirely likely that they may not even result in his being a better manager. It is quite possible that the personal possession (or arrogation) of such extreme qualities, particularly in a cooperative organizational setting, will cloud his perception, and degrade his ability to manage the organization.

However, the purpose of this book is not merely to restate the admonition that pride comes before a fall, however much it evidently bears repeating. In the present context, the intent of this book is twofold: to contribute to the restoration of management to its proper place at the apex of the organization, and also to place the definition of leadership—not back into the definition of management—but, rather, back into its proper place as an integral characteristic of the organization itself.

The Group Spirit

The pioneering social psychologist Kurt Lewin described people as existing in *force fields*, which emanated from their social, organizational, familial, and other environmental surroundings. He argued that these can be driving, restraining, or, essentially, neutral forces. Driving forces impel people toward certain actions. He identified these as those oriented toward change, but the basic idea of open-minded dynamism is the fundamental concept. In a group context, these forces bring into being countervailing restraining forces, which actively inhibit, or even suppress, such behaviors. The neutral forces have no effect on the impulse to engage in or avoid change or dynamism in the group. Lewin understood this environmental brew of forces to be itself dynamic, changing, and evolving into and out of equilibrium. He developed a model for creating organizational change based on analysis of the driving and restraining forces in a group, and their manipulation in a manner designed to effect the desired outcome.

What is of interest here is his insight that we are individually woven into a web of forces that arise not from our sense of ourselves individually, but from the group and its sense of itself as an independent entity. In the context of the present discussion, we will see that we both influence and are influenced by these forces. Even when the driving and restraining forces are in equilibrium, the neutral forces may be altered by us, or by external events, into actively influential forces with respect to driving or restraining organizational dynamism or change. That is, like Marshall's soldiers who are nonshooters in one engagement, they may become shooters in the next, depending on the confluence of their abilities, their locations in the organization, and its intersection with the external environment. Further, like Marshall's nonshooters, who nevertheless contribute to the morale of the unit by their very presence, and who support change by adapting themselves to it and evolving along with its expression, the neutral forces may be viewed substantially as stoically supportive forces of the existence of the organization, itself. The components of these neutral forces may be neutral at any given time with respect to issues of change or dynamism confronting the organization. Their very presence, however, both supports the coherence of the organization, and emboldens the constructive dialogue and activity of the driving and restraining forces. The neutral forces, viewed in this light, may be seen as lending a sort of organizational inertia or momentum to the outcome of the dialogue, whether it results in equilibrium, change, or even a retreat from change.

Lewin described a method for promoting organizational change by unfreezing, changing, and refreezing the stasis by which the driving and restraining forces in the group might have become captured. Lewin described some of these forces as ambitions, fears, or needs, leading to the promotion of, or resistance to, change by the organization and its individuals. However, they also lead to the expression of, and response to, leadership by the organization and its individuals. These forces influence the way opportunities and threats are perceived by the organization and its members, and how they respond to or influence them.

The Guiding Force

Lewin also conducted an important study, in which he observed three leadership styles used among groups of boys at play. He referred to these as the democratic, autocratic, and laissez-faire styles. He observed that the group led by an autocratic leader experienced extremes of aggressive or apathetic behavior by its members, and that there was a general environment of discontent. The democratic group saw both more general satisfaction, and more proactive involvement by all the participants in the group's activities. The laissez-faire group was neither particularly content nor discontented, and it was less active and less effective at producing or reaching group goals.

Lewin went further. He taught the leaders the other styles, and had them alternate the use of those styles with their groups. He found that the characteristics of the group, as described above, changed according to the style of leadership used—notwithstanding that the same individual was still the leader. Various lessons were drawn from these studies, ranging from the notion that the democratic style was generally preferable, to the idea that leaders can learn to modify their leadership styles and to successfully employ improved leadership techniques.

Here, we will look at the parallels between Lewin's observations of groups which were led according to the three leadership styles, and his three general forces operating on people in groups. The association between laissez-faire leadership and neutral forces would appear to be obvious. Neither promotes any particular agenda; each appears to be more or less content with, and amenable to, whatever comes down the road. Regarding the others, there may be a temptation to associate positive attributes to the democratic leadership style and to the driving force, and to pair them together. Furthermore, we may be inclined to attribute negative attributes to the pair of autocratic style and restraining force. This is neither necessarily useful nor appropriate. Without ascribing particular virtues to them, it is sufficient to propose that the similarity between the democratic leadership style and the driving forces is that there is a general tendency for them to promote involvement and engagement in the issues addressing the organization. The autocratic style and the restraining forces, on the other hand, can be argued to tend to encourage the disengagement of the individual from issues facing the organization, leaving those issues either intentionally (autocratic leadership) or perhaps by default (restraining forces) to the attention of others.

Now, let us take a closer look at each of the leadership approaches. The laissez-faire style would appear, on the face of it, to be more or less in accord with the thesis of this book that organizations generate their own leadership. However, the phenomenon of leadership self-generating within an organization should not be viewed as inevitably positive or constructive. Leaving an organization's leadership to its own devices does not guarantee a rewarding outcome from the viewpoint of those who own, or are responsible for, the organization. Without that organizational leadership itself being guided and managed, it can produce results ranging from beneficial to damaging. Simply creating a group and leaving it to organize itself could well lead to the organizational decks teeming with loose cannons, careening about and causing unpredictable mayhem. This book, in arguing that leadership arises from the organization, does not propose that the organization be abandoned to that leadership. Leadership needs to be managed. A group led by a laissez-faire style may be viewed as having its fate placed in the hands of the neutral forces. However, these forces are not inherently focused on the opportunities and threats facing the organization, on the contemplation—whether for or against—of action. They merely act as a kind of gravity, helping to form the basis of the organization's group cohesion. They may, depending on circumstances, evolve into more proactive forces. But then again, they may not. To adopt such a leadership style is, essentially, akin to leaving the organization's fate to chance.

The autocratic style, for its part, arrogates to the leader all responsibility for the inspiration, mobilization, organization, and operation of the group. In other words, this is the perfect vehicle for he who subscribes to the theory that organizations are led by the senior executive at the top, rather than managed by him. He is the source of the leadership functions, and the organization is his tool for expressing them. We will not repeat here the problems with this view, both for the individual leader and the organization, as these are outlined in the first two chapters of this book. The autocratic style has the tendency to draw the focus to the leader and his abilities and intentions, and not those of the organization. This further tends to cause the leader to misapprehend his relationship with the organization, and to confuse the issue of which serves which. Additionally, it also detaches the individual employee from the organization. The natural tendency of adults to seek ways to contribute meaningfully to their surroundings is frustrated by the autocratic ethic, which suggests that all meaningful ideas and inspirations will come from above, and that the role of the employee is to await and then express them. This leads to the anger and the apathy that Lewin identified. This style both ignores and frustrates the natural expression of leadership, and disengages the neutral forces of stoic support that form the basis of group cohesion. These forces will still exist as long as the individuals continue to assemble in the organizational setting, but they will begin to operate by developing cohesion around some manner of group identification that is progressively more removed from the organization itself—at least, as it is understood by its owners. The force that comes to the fore, however, will be Lewin's restraining force, inhibiting or suppressing individual investment in the endeavor's dynamism. Employees in such environments tend generally to be reactive, not proactive.

The democratic style appears to have attributes that create useful dynamics within the group. The participants enjoy their membership, they are involved, and they appear to be productive. Lewin's hope had been to prove, in addition to the idea that leadership could be taught, that the democratic style was the preferred approach. While that is a topic that warrants discussion, it is not the topic of this book. We are interested here in how leadership functions in an organization, and how to marshal it in a manner that helps the organization to better accomplish its goals. Lewin's observations about the effects in the group of the democratic approach are of interest, here, because they show the active interest of the group being drawn out and directed to the purpose of the group. The comparison with Lewin's driving force is the creation of an organizational energy predisposed to dynamism and the willingness to risk taking action. Again, it is difficult today to avoid associating positive connotations with the characteristics of democracy, the ideal of content and engaged employees, dynamism, and a bias for action. However, it is useful to note that organizations are not typically created to exhibit any particular leadership style, provide any particular degree of involvement or self-actualization to their employees, or to have a bias for action or anything else that is not ineluctably related to the accomplishment of the organization's mission. Therefore, it is not in any virtues presumed to be inherent in democratic leadership of organizations, or in the supposedly positive features of the directing forces, that we are interested. It is to whatever helps us to identify, draw out, and mobilize the phenomenon of leadership in the organization to its advantage, that we wish to focus our attention. As it turns out, of the three styles observed by Lewin, the democratic style seems to be the one that best accomplishes this end. What is there to be learned in this finding?

Marshaling the Forces

Lewin wanted to promote the democratic leadership style as the best means of running organizations. We argue here that, while the end does not justify any means, it is only the end result that is the proper concern of the manager of an organization. The observation that engaged, involved employees, and dynamic organizational environments, tend to support achievement of this result should not obscure the importance of the proper placement of the focus of attention of the senior executive. It is important to understand which is the consequence of which. It is clearly understood, today, that contented employees engaged in a dynamic environment are capable of helping organizations to achieve positive results. Nevertheless, where this is the case, from the perspective of the organization, the contentment of the employees is the means, not the end. It is not that an organization's executives should not wish to have, or to take pride, in such work forces. It is that they should clearly remember that the relationship between employee self-fulfillment, and organizational health and survival, is fueled by the latter. Failure to provide the latter will lead to failure to provide either.

With this in mind, we can take another look at the pairings of Lewin's democratic leadership style and dynamic forces. The key insight is the very presence of such forces in an organization. Lewin used his concept of the three general types of forces to develop a theory of organizational change, and a model for enabling it. The real value, however, is in attracting managerial attention to the presence of these forces. Recognizing that they tend to contribute to group attitudes toward such things as change does not go far enough in acknowledging their potential importance. In addition to forming a setting within which group cohesion can take place, they actually are expressions of a group consciousness in the organization and a collective attention to issues of concern to it. This is distinct from the effects of these forces on individuals within the organization, although the individuals, and the forces set in motion by their assemblage in the organizational setting, influence each other. The forces would not exist as they do outside of the organization. They cause fundamental shifts in the way individuals perceive and interpret events that are of interest—not to them as individuals—but to the organization. It is in the combination of the collective sense of identification made possible by these forces, and the collective nature of the individual interaction in the organization through the medium they generate, that is of interest to the manager. It is this combination that provides the possibility of the creation of group cohesion, and it is from group cohesion that individual expressions of organizational leadership arise.

There is nothing particularly profound or inscrutable about this. One's perspective changes when one joins a group, whether a friendship, a marriage or family, a military unit, religious community—any type of organization. The individual begins to feel and be affected by things that do not necessarily concern him as an individual. He senses and is concerned about things that act on others in the group. This phenomenon experienced by him and the other individuals in the group gives rise to the forces that begin to act on the group as a whole. Some of these forces are individual drives that take on new characteristics in the organizational setting, and others are peculiar to the organization. The individual begins to identify with the other individuals in the group, and, progressively, to identify more with the group itself. He perceives and anticipates the opportunities and needs of not merely the other individuals who happen to have found themselves with him in the group, but of the group as a distinct entity. This is what gives rise to the basic environment from which group cohesion develops. It is from group cohesion that arise spontaneous individual expressions of the various forms of organizational leadership. The strength of this phenomenon more or less corresponds with the strength of the cohesion of the group.

This is what managers want to concern themselves with. It is sufficient to be aware that the potential for the development of group cohesion arises when people are assembled in an organization for the pursuit of a common aim. From that arises organizational leadership expressed from within the organization by its members. In Lewin's laissez-faire organization, group cohesion is never really sparked into actionable existence. In the autocratically led system, group cohesion is suppressed or tamed. Expression of individual initiative is perceived as threatening, and it is repressed. Group cohesion dissolves in an environment where concern for others is viewed as an untoward interpositioning of one's self between the employees and the autocratic leadership, and concern for the group as such is not rewarded. Every man for himself.

Lewin observed that, in his democratically led groups, there was group-member satisfaction and cooperative engagement and involvement. This indicates the presence of group cohesion. The involvement was participative. This suggests organizational leadership expressed from within the group. This led to productive activity by the group. This, of course, is the aim of the manager.

United in Spirit

During his observations of men in combat reported in *Men Against Fire*, Marshall noted that most of the soldiers who were able to steel themselves to take proactive measures against—in particular, to open fire on—enemy soldiers, were crew-served weapons men. These are teams of men who employ weapons that cannot be carried and operated by a single soldier. The rifle carried by the typical front line soldier is not a crew-served weapon. However, machine guns and mortars are. Small groups of men were trained to maintain, transport, deploy, and operate these weapons. Special training and teamwork were required to coordinate the preparations, activities, and follow-on measures taken by the crewmembers, as individuals and as a crew, to enable their valuable weapons to be successfully employed in a highly dangerous environment, and to advance the cause of the unit.

We have seen how individual soldiers on the line can, at the commencement of combat, appear to lose direct contact with, and intimate awareness of, their fellows and of the situation generally, becoming stoic but passive supporters of the unit's activities. But the men in a crew-served weapon team were intently aware of the contribution of their individual actions on the others in their crew, on the ability of the weapon to be deployed against the enemy, and thus on the fate of the unit as a whole. Moreover, when enemy fire opened up and they hit the deck, they were not isolated like the line infantryman. They were together. Perhaps as they looked at each other, they held with each other a silent version of Captain Williams's dialogue with his fellow officer and his radioman: "What do we do now?" "We're ready when you are." As a result, Marshall noted that not only were the crews on such weapons generally to be counted among the active shooters in combat, but, if their weapons went out of action for whatever reason, they didn't stop. They found other weapons, or other means of continuing the action.

The forces that bind together such teams are powerful, and become more so under the stress of the performance of their unique and important mission. The group cohesion is strong, and becomes a fierce medium of group awareness, spontaneously generating unspoken individual expressions of its own leadership in a dynamic fashion which adapts to the evolving circumstances in an effort to accomplish its tasks. This is all the more so when the group cohesion of the team is reinforced by cohesion with the larger group.

As noted previously, the business world has taken this lesson. The use of teams in all sorts of organizations has become an industry in its own right, rivaling that of the modern individual leadership movement. There are similar excesses in the modern team movement. Teams are identified as the answer to every organizational problem. Some proponents even argue that organizations should be designed around them. The principal failing here is that the effect is confused for the cause. Powerful dynamism, loyalty, creativity, and achievement are not attained simply by organizing individuals into small groups. The dynamic group cohesion and organizational leadership generated by teams occurs when there is a clear need for a group of individuals to perform, as a team, a task that is of distinct value and importance to the larger group. This is what generates the group cohesion and proactive involvement of the team's members. Further, the connection with the larger group, provided by the importance of the task, supports the integrity of the arrangement and deepens the endurance and resilience of the process. Attempts to produce the benefits of teams where these conditions do not exist are generally recognized by employees as ineffectual and inept efforts to manipulate them. For the present discussion, a key value of the phenomenon of teams is the clear and focused example they provide of how group cohesion generates powerful *field forces*, as Lewin might describe them, within the teams, which in turn generate leadership. Additionally, they provide a lesson about how the force of the leadership is related to the intensity of the cohesion, which is itself related to the basic integrity and perceived value and importance of the structural arrangement and organizational purpose of the team.

It is useful, then, for the manager to identify the organizational characteristic of leadership as inherent in the organization itself. Thus, it can be seen that it is an asset like any other available or organic to the organization. It can be identified, analyzed, cultivated, and deployed in the service of the organization. How this might be done will be discussed in the next chapter. Here, we will conclude with a brief discussion of the nature of the senior executive who makes it happen.

CAPTAINS OF INDUSTRY

To begin with, the person who makes this happen is not the leader in the sense meant by the modern leadership movement. No single person typically performs, nor consistently can effectively exhibit, the leadership functions for an organization. Those who attempt to do so, aside from demonstrating an almost certainly unwarranted confidence in themselves, are also demonstrating a lack of it in others. One who feels that he is, or must continuously be seen to be, a superior individual leader in contrast to other potential contenders for that title is likely to reject the good intentions and judgment of others, as well. The resultant pressures and strains he places on himself will almost certainly destroy, or severely damage, his well being—and that of his organization along with him.

Even if he is able to exhibit, or merely able to convince others that he is exhibiting, truly superior individual leadership, this very performance, delivered this way, will tend to undermine the vitality and durability of the organization. Anyone who is familiar with sports knows that teamwork is more important than any single person's ability, and that the display of individual brilliance at the expense of the potential contributions of others and of the exponential value of teamwork will, over time, degrade, and even destroy, the performance of the team. This applies in organizations as well.

Arrogation of leadership to himself by the senior executive acts to suppress the generally superior instances of it available in, and seeking routes for expression from within, the organization. That is to say, it is not strictly necessary for him to display leadership in the technical sense, at all. It is already inherent in the organization and, properly managed, can be brought productively to bear on the activities of the organization at the cost of much less individual and organizational anxiety and stress than is generally caused by the "great leaders" of today's leadership movement.

Properly understood then, the organization's leaders do not belong, and are not to be found, at the top of the organization. They are to be found within it. At the top is the real boss, the true captain of industry. At the top is the manager.

Know Thyself

We have seen the lofty traits attributed by the modern leadership movement to the individual leader. Preemptively dismissing calls for access and inclusion with throw-away lines about how anyone can be a leader, the movement's proponents then go on to ascribe to leaders the most singular moral, technical, and visionary abilities. If anyone can be such a leader, then all of us can not only be above average—we can be extraordinary human beings.

The truth is, however, that such individuals are, at the very least, in short supply. Even should we locate someone presumed to be such an individual, we would likely be courting disaster for our organization by placing him at the head of it.

One of the taskings assigned these individuals by their mentors in the leadership movement, is the requirement to take periodic spiritual inner journeys, in order to confront their demons, test their moral mettle, and learn who they are. I have argued that the examined life is a virtue in and of itself, and no more so for a leader at the top than for a leader within the organization. One's inner journeys had best begin long before reaching the top. What's more, if someone is undertaking such a journey in the conscious endeavor to facilitate getting to, or staying at, the top, then he is still living a fundamentally unexamined, and even hypocritical, life. Furthermore, to suggest that such journeys to self-knowledge and moral development are of greater value to those at the top than to those within the organization is revealing enough about the personal character and judgment of those who pretend to take them.

Still, are there no distinguishing characteristics at all required of one who would manage a large organization? Are there no special or unique attributes that he should possess or develop? How can such a manager or his duties be described?

As mentioned in the preface, this book rejects the thesis in Emerson's statement that an organization is the lengthened shadow of its leader. However, in the military, it is recognized that a unit's attitude and morale are a *reflection* of its *commander*. The commander sets the organizational and operational tone of the unit in ways that are felt throughout. It can be striking to see how rapidly a unit's atmosphere changes to reflect the personality of a new boss. This is not a consequence of some monolithic directive style of military organizational behavior. It is a consequence of the personal characteristics and managerial systems employed by a diverse body of commanders. This is the case in civilian organizations as well.

While so-called leadership traits, such as integrity, technical competence, and loyalty, are taught in the military, they are taught to, and expected of, everyone. Not just the generals, but also the privates. As a rule, the absence of these traits does not disqualify one merely from promotion, but from continued service as well. Neither is it the possession of such qualities by themselves that leads to high command. Rather, it is the possession of certain qualities of *command*, or *command presence*, which leads the way to the top.

It is this characteristic of command that enables managers to understand their organizations, draw out the strengths within them, including leadership, and deploy them to the benefit of the organization. A detailed discussion of the qualities of command is beyond the scope of this book. It is sufficient here to say that it is an acknowledgment, not of privilege or individual accomplishment, but of responsibility, and the ability to draw accomplishment from others.

Some might view this as the ability to inspire, which is often touted as one of the unique characteristics of a leader. Yet it is fundamentally a managerial skill to instill in the organization its meaning for existing and a respect for individual contribution to that meaning. This lies at the heart of the marshaling and management of assets, be they material or moral. The manager does so, not to display artistry or personal skill, but to draw those from the organization for its benefit.

There is no particular advantage for a senior executive or his organization to his adopting poses, or delivering uncalled-for and reckless displays of virtuosity or daring. Such performances will be seen as self-serving, basically fraudulent, and dismissive of the contributions of the organization by those within it.

On the contrary, the singularly essential characteristic of the manager who is a successful commander is the ability to focus on the tasks at hand, think lucidly and objectively about them, and to work hard to address them. That, by itself, will go a long way toward signaling to the organization and its members the essential value of what they do, and the virtue of its being done. It will begin the generation of cohesion and loyalty to the organization.

Regarding loyalty, the manager cannot require it. It cannot be characterized as a necessary ingredient of organizational membership or advancement. Such prescriptions are reflective of autocratic systems, and are all but guaranteed to produce, instead, bitterness, cynicism, and apathy. Loyalty is earned, not demanded. It is given to those managers who show to the organization their own devotion to organizational goals, willingness to work hard to accomplish them, and to learn from all how to do so. The manager who attracts the greatest loyalty is not he who displays superior skills or flair, but he who earns the confidence of his employees in his faith in the value of what he and they are doing, and who will work hard, honestly, and fairly to help them all do it better.

Management of organizational leadership is not a consciousness-raising exercise. Nor is it a consensus system leading to ponderous decision-making, or designed to create a particular sort of work environment. Management of organizational leadership can take place effectively across a wide range of managerial styles, and in a wide range of operational circumstances. It is characterized by clear-thinking decisiveness that identifies and employs all assets available to it, including the leadership inherent in the organization itself.

That leadership arises naturally from the group cohesion of the organization. It is generated by, but is distinct from, the assembly together of individuals for engaging in a collective enterprise. That is, it is not merely the combined aspirations of these individuals for the group, and for themselves in it. Rather, it produces perspectives, insights, and compulsions to act, or to support actions, that serve the interests of the collaborative organization. These would not otherwise appear in its individuals were they not embedded in the group cohesion arising from their collective endeavor. Similar to Lewin's force fields, the organizational leadership produced, and within which the group's members operate, causes them to take on extra-individual concern for the organization and its members. It communicates itself among them and anticipates, creates, and responds to individual expressions of itself throughout the organization. It expects, demands, generates, distributes, and adapts itself to leadership wherever in the organization it determines it may be needed.

It is time now to turn to a discussion of how managers can manage that extraordinary asset. In the next chapter, we will review some of the principal functions of leadership, and examine methods for managers to draw more effective expressions of leadership from within the organization than they could hope to deliver themselves.

7

Managing Leadership

o o o o o o o o o o o o o o o o o o o o o o o o o o o o o o o o o
"Nearly all men can stand adversity,
but if you want to test a man's character,
give him power."

—*Abraham Lincoln*

In the mid-1980s, one of the articles routinely making the reading list in management classes was written by a business journalist about an interview he had conducted.[12] He had asked a local company who they recommended for the interview, and they referred him to the manager of a bottling plant. This manager had made the plant into a reliable and efficient profit center, and the junior managers on his staff consistently went on to become star performers in the company. The journalist called the plant and the manager picked up the phone. A little startled at immediately getting the top man, he asked for an interview. "Sure," the manager said. "Come on over." The journalist asked for an appointment, and he was told just to come over any time. But not on Thursdays—that was the day the manager went golfing, or on other social events, with local community notables. And not on Wednesday mornings—that was when he held his weekly staff meeting. A little hesitantly, the journalist showed up at the plant one day and was welcomed by the manager in his simple, uncluttered office. The journalist asked how such a successful manager could have such an open schedule and peaceful office environment. Why was such a plant, known for producing both exceptional profits and managers, not humming with activity and dynamism?

The manager explained his system, which, in summary, was as follows. Each of his junior managers headed a different department of the plant—operations, supply, finance, and so on. They ran daily operations, and also made sure they had anticipated and prepared for any unusual future events. These included not only seasonal fluctuations, but also competitor activity and technological advances that might affect productivity, and the like. The junior managers may or may not hold regular or periodic meetings—that was up to them. However, they were required by the manager to run the plant smoothly and efficiently, and to solve or respond appropriately to all problems and opportunities encountered.

For his part, the manager spent most of his time maintaining positive relations with the local community, keeping an eye on events or trends in the general company-wide and external environments that affected his plant, and planning ahead. His involvement in the day-to-day affairs of the plant consisted of two things. First, once a week, the plant's data systems delivered to the printer in his office the fundamental operational and financial data he used to ascertain the status of the plant and the efficiency of its operations. This data was not extensive or complex, and it did not intricately elaborate the condition of the plant. It was simple and concise, and pointed in a robust and unmistakable way to the plant's fundamental health. Second, he chaired the weekly Wednesday morning staff meeting.

At this weekly meeting each junior manager was obliged to describe the issues he had encountered during the past week, and what he had done, or was doing, about them. He was not allowed to ask the manager for help, but simply to report the issue, his analysis of it, and how he was doing with it. Further, he was required to identify any of the other junior managers who had helped him with the issue. Failure to report any legitimately rendered help would result in a severe reprimand and notation in the manager's file. The ethic of the staff was such that a failure by one who had been helped to report that, would usually be tactfully pointed out right at the staff meeting by a third party manager who knew of the incident but was not involved in it. While these mechanisms and sanctions were in place, and it was clear to all that they would be exercised, this was not found to be necessary. Everyone reported fully any assistance received and there was no evidence that anyone tried to take credit for specific solutions that they had not generated themselves. While they were required to give credit where it was due for particular ideas or advice received, they personally retained overall credit for the resolution of the issue facing their department.

The manager chaired the meeting, but did not appear to actively contribute to it. He did not deliver guidance or directives. He might pass along company or environmental news affecting the plant, or propose ideas to think about, or areas to keep an eye on, based on his scans of the company's internal and external environments. However, he did not interfere, where not necessary, in the manner in which his junior managers carried out his policies for their discharge of their duties, and their interaction in running the plant. He did always make notes regarding which junior managers had been cited for providing helpful advice and assistance. Whenever the manager was unable to chair the weekly meeting, or to attend other obligatory company events, due to business travel or vacations, the most-cited junior was assigned to act in his place.

The manager explained that many of his peers felt that they had to validate their own positions as head executive in their plants by demonstrating superiority over their juniors in every area. Further, they felt a need to be more creative and more knowledgeable about the company, and encouraged their junior managers to seek them out for help in resolving issues that came up in their departments. The manager explained to the journalist that he felt that this prevented the junior managers from developing self-confidence, self-reliance, and teamwork. It undermined their credibility with their own staffs, and was based on the unlikely, and perishable, assumption that the manager was better acquainted with their daily operations than they were themselves. He felt his system better addressed all those issues, and that the success enjoyed by his plant, and his managers in the company after graduating from his system, validated this. Further, it freed him to concentrate on tasks that were more appropriate to his actual responsibilities.

Clearly, this manager did not arrogate to himself all the leadership and management functions of the organization. His style was certainly not autocratic, but neither was it laissez-faire, or even democratic. Matters were not simply left to the staff—there were clearly stated targets to be hit. Further, while he delegated authority, he clearly retained responsibility, and would step in and take control if and when necessary. However, when it was not—and it hardly ever was—he would allow the natural abilities and instincts of his organization and its members and managers to develop and to run things.

Consciously aware of it or not, this manager built on the basic materials of group cohesion available in any organization. He created a managerial environment where those materials strengthened and generated an organizational leadership consciousness, and individual expressions of leadership, that were efficiently directed to the goals of the organization. His story makes for an intriguing introduction to this chapter about managing the leadership inherent in the organization. After all, this manager did not develop the most profitable plant and the most successful junior manager training program in his company by arrogating to himself the principal leadership role in these endeavors. He did it by cultivating, harnessing, and deploying the leadership assets inherent in the organization.

An exhaustive examination of how to manage organizational leadership generated from within is an intricate and involved effort that cannot be adequately addressed within the broader purpose of this book. Nevertheless, in this chapter, we will build on this manager's example to review some basic principles and methods that any manager, in any setting, might use to manage the leadership in his organization.

PURPOSE

One instance in which leadership occurs outside the organization is at its birth. Organizations are created to accomplish tasks that are too great in scope, time, or demand for resources for one person to accomplish. Those tasks have to be conceived of before the organization is created to accomplish them. In fact, the conception of such a great enterprise as to require the creation of an organization to pursue it is often identified as the quintessential example of individual leadership. Often, the exemplars are of lofty purposes, such as the discovery of new territories on earth or in space, surmounting presumed limits on human capabilities, or creating new technologies for the betterment of mankind. However, it is not necessary that the inspiration for an organizational effort be breathtaking for it to be counted as leadership, or to bring forth an organization to pursue it. Perfectly ordinary or common endeavors pursued by organizations are just as much the result of inspiration and vision, and no more or less so than those that capture the attention of a wider audience. At some point, someone determines to do something in a certain way, and in one form or another, this determination draws and organizes people in its pursuit.

Once the organization is in place, however, we have a new situation. We now have a tension between leading and managing it. Some refer to the early years of a new organization as the entrepreneurial age, when the founder continues to personally lead it. If it succeeds in achieving a certain degree of growth, the time comes to turn it over to professional management. This is probably an acceptable description of the process of the transfer of an organization's operation from the leadership of its founder to professional management. The period of control by the founding leader may or may not be turbulent, but it is the founder's or owner's inherent right to lead the organization as he wishes or is inclined. The consequences of his decisions in this regard will be communicated directly to him through his invested capital. It is when the professional successor attempts to supplant management of the organization with leadership of it, as propounded by the modern leadership movement, that real problems can begin to surface. The hired manager does not have the degree of accountability required to legitimately authorize him to impose his own inspirations or vision for the organization on it or its owners. The fact that the modern leadership phenomenon has resulted in the moral disenfranchisement of boards, enabling hired hands to impose owner-like control over our organizations, is a major reason why we have experienced so many negative results from their leadership. The accountability gap between derived authority and the assumption of functions only legitimately expressed by those with direct responsibility[13] gives rise to insuperable moral hazard. Among the instances where this occurs is when those without direct founding leadership responsibility nevertheless arrogate to themselves the ability to exhibit that level of control over the inspirational vision and direction of the organization.

The potential for organizational leadership from within develops after the initial insight that generates the creation of the organization. The question of the efficacy of individual leadership expressed beyond that point is distinct from that of the legitimacy of individual leadership. The exhibition by owners of the individual leadership style of running their company can be criticized on many of the same bases as has been done in this book. It cannot, however, be denounced as fundamentally illegitimate. When done by hired managers, it can.

We will presume here, then, that we are dealing with an organization managed by contracted professionals. Such an organization's managers will receive their remit from the owners through the appropriate vehicle, typically a board. Any thoughts of the vision of what the organization is, or ought to become, should be communicated to management by its owners, or recommended to the latter by management. It should then be approved and formally recommunicated by the owners to management. The first instance of inspirational vision for the organization, however, is what leads to its birth.

Scanning

The general area of ensuring the provision of an appropriate general direction for an organization is generally viewed as a—perhaps, the—proper sphere of activity of senior management. Our bottling plant manager seemed to think so. Even Mary Follett, who felt that the management of an organization could not effectively come from only above, believed that attempting to discern the future, and prepare the organization for it, was a special duty of top management; she even described this as the special vision of the leader.

Effective senior managers delegate what is not appropriately done by them to those closer to the issues, reserving to themselves the establishment of direction and policy. The problem is that they rarely are able to devote adequate time to such tasks, since so much of their attention is unavoidably drawn by the immediate demands of customers, events in the surrounding business and community environments, and events in their own organizations. Fortunately, however, even the establishment of direction and policy need not be done exclusively by senior managers. Where there is strong group cohesion, there will be the potential for the organization, as a whole, to help shoulder this burden, and enable it to be considered from a broader and more comprehensive perspective than it might otherwise. Marshall's soldiers were only taught how to perform fire and movement, but, in the stress of combat, some of them found that they had instinctive insights about what effects the unfolding of events in their vicinity would have on their units. Civilian organizations can be taught to be alert to this as well.

Virtually all of the organization's employees, whether in production, sales and customer relations, or supply and logistics, are at one or another important interface of the organization with its markets, suppliers, distributors, retailers, or general business or community environments. These employees are scouts, and they see discrete events and trends that may be important to the organization. More significantly, they are likely to be the first to observe the indicators of changes in trends, which are far more significant to an organization than merely the measurement of current trends. Managers need to examine their organizations to learn how they can alert their employees to their value in this area, and how to set up systems and procedures for collecting and processing the data generated by them.

In the press of day-to-day events, such efforts at generating effective foresight tend to be bumped down the priority list. When it comes time to set the next plan, or when it becomes clear that something is rendering the current organizational view of the world untenable, it is too late to expect the special vision of the leader to save the day. He has been harassed, himself, by a multitude of demands not even typically viewed as appropriate to his position, but which cannot be avoided and cannot be delegated. He cannot come up with a balanced assessment, or a vision, under a short deadline, and while an outside perspective is a helpful aid to the process, it is generally unwise to outsource the process itself. Even if the senior executive did have the unique ability to retain control of his time, it would probably be best for him not to use it to take inner journeys, or lock himself away to think in philosophic isolation, in order to emerge as the leader with the special vision. While the perspective of the troops on the line has its own limitations and shortcomings, so does that of a top management isolated from the way the organization sees the world from the multiple perspectives of its employees. The solution is for management to harness and deploy the powerful organizational leadership resources available to it to develop a comprehensive and widely informed view of the organization's unique character, capabilities, and environment.

Vision

Which often brings the topic back to the vision of the organization—what it is, and what is its function in the marketplace. For example, much has been made of the disappearance of horse-drawn carriage makers when the automobile came on the scene. It would have appeared that they understood much that was useful about building what were, essentially, cars; it would have been logical for them to adopt the new technology and transform themselves into the automobile industry. They didn't because they did not see themselves more generally as companies that made means of transport—they saw themselves, simply, as horse-drawn carriage makers.

Employees are generally just as prone to this sort of habitual thought as are managers. However, they are also much closer to the various markets where the organization operates. They should be trained to keep an eye not only on when, why, and how trends are changing in those markets, but also on how the organization's various external interlocutors perceive it. Dialogues such as this with customers, vendors, and others may provide life-saving insights into, not only how the organization can most efficiently and effectively serve its customers, but also into what they think the organization really is. In the past few decades, the managers of many companies have developed reinventions of their organizations, and tried to sell these new visions to their markets, with mixed results that are costly even when ultimately successful. It is easier to let your customers tell you who you are. Moreover, it is your employees who often are in the best position to detect when your customers, and other interlocutors, are sending signals about that which do not coincide with what the organization understands itself to actually be. The employees often are also good judges of which of these signals should be given what degree of weight.

In such an event, senior management should not only draw on the natural inclination of the employees to observe the environment from the organizational perspective, but should also draw on their instinct to understand the implications for the organization of those observations. When such a profound and comprehensive reassessment of the organization's identity is developed, management has a viable and credible proposal to take to the board for a formal reconsideration of the organizational vision.

Planning

Plans of various time ranges are typically generated by senior management, shorter ranges extrapolated from longer ranges, and the results converted to goals that can be transmitted to subordinate units and measured for progress. Additional plans are then generated in the subunits to accomplish the assigned goals. Sometimes, although far from as often as is appropriate, it is in the subunit goal planning that unit employees are, wisely, brought into the process, to one degree or another.

Our focus, however, is on the senior management, the phenomenon of the self-generation of leadership from within the organization, and the potential this presents to avoid placing the destructive burden on the senior executive, and on the organization, of the modern notions of comprehensively charismatic individual leadership. The thesis is that senior management is superior to the leadership exhibited at any level in the organization, and that its duty is to appropriately cultivate and deploy this leadership to advance the aim of the organization. This can be accomplished to the benefit of planning at the highest levels, as well. Further, it is another important instance of helping to ensure that the highest level planning, from which all other plans and goals are derived, does not become the blunted product of groupthink or isolation.

As it happens, however, strategic planning is clearly the reserve of senior management. In fact, that, and high-level decision-making, are arguably the two enterprises that can legitimately be performed only by managers, and not delegated, or left to be self-generated, or, somehow, to take shape of their own accord from within the organization. However, that does not strictly exclude the participation of the organization. The most critical—and most poorly executed—element of planning or decision-making is the process of framing the issue. Any senior management, however, that is cultivating and employing the leadership instincts, inherent to the organization, of seeking to observe and understand the environment, has gone a long way toward providing for, and safeguarding, the perspective and integrity of the issue-framing process. When done in isolation by top management, on the other hand, it runs a much higher risk of being hijacked by the agendas of internal power blocks or external consultants, or simply being hamstrung by groupthink. When the expressions of these leadership functions by the whole organization have been properly mobilized and managed, senior executives are generally in a much better position, and more broadly informed state of mind, to undertake their unique duty of strategic planning. Furthermore, it is precisely good, solid, well conceived, and thoroughly thought-out strategic planning that we should expect from senior management—not the sort of flashy, publicity-generating tactics that pass for strategic thinking in many organizations. Operations and tactics should be left to lower levels of management, and to the organization itself.

ORGANIZATION

When an endeavor too large for one person is undertaken, people are assembled into organizations in order to pursue it. Simply doing that, however, is not enough. The organization itself needs to be organized in a fashion that facilitates the accomplishment of the purposes that gave rise to it. The design of the organization begins with the processes that will produce the desired organizational outcome. The conception and design of these processes themselves may represent extraordinary ability or intellect. However, the organizational design is generally intended to reduce the execution of these processes into ordered routines that can be performed by any adequately trained employee.

What's more, the design of the organization, in addition to making the production process routine, should also make the management of the organization routine. The shape, function, communication pathways, and locations of the organization's parts should take as much as possible of the burden of day-to-day management off the shoulders of its managers. Generally, it should require the presence of geniuses neither among its employees nor among its management. Certainly, a genius might be helpful in certain research functions, but even those can generally produce results if they are well conceived and operated, and relentlessly pursued. However, an organization that requires genius on a daily basis to produce its output, or to manage itself, is almost certainly poorly organized.

Further, it is typically in an independent setting that genius is creative. In an organization, it can be destructive, particularly when it somehow is seen to supplant ordinary organizational functions. Any brilliant individual performance in a team setting, if continued heedlessly and unnecessarily, will undermine the team setting itself, and can leave the group dangerously underperforming when, as it inevitably will, the genius runs out of inspiration. While we certainly want, and need not settle for less than, skilled and talented executives, organizations should be designed as much as possible to enable them to be run by average, hard-working managers. Best of all, they should practically be capable of running themselves. We will look, from just a couple of perspectives, at ways in which a properly organized organization might take advantage of the leadership it generates from within.

Mobilizing

An organization identifies and mobilizes assets for deployment in pursuit of the organizational purpose. These assets include the organization's human resources, and these include the phenomenon of organizational leadership. This leadership, contributing as it does to the expression of the functions of leadership, also contributes to the mobilization of resources. In pursuit of an organizational objective, those employees who perceive opportunities for productive action, and those who act on the opportunities, have identified some form of asset that can be employed to the organization's advantage, and they have taken steps to benefit from it. This may be a peculiar means of publicizing the organizational objective, in which case an employee will have found a way to get external media or public relations agencies to aid in marketing the organization's products, or preparing the way for new initiatives. Similarly, it could be a new method of involving vendors or distributors in enhancing the organization's competitive position. In either sort of situation, such an employee initiative will have extended organizational assets beyond those possessed and controlled directly by the organization. Certainly, it is at least as likely that an employee may discover a new way of employing existing assets, or organizing existing processes. Whether participating in the mobilization of internal or external assets, however, the employee will have generated the mobilization of resources for the benefit of the organization. Furthermore, the initiative-taking employee will have made an advance. When that advance is assessed as advantageous by the organization as a whole, through the medium of its core stoic supporters, they will begin the process of moving alongside of the new initiative and adjusting themselves, and the organization itself, to the new process or procedure.

Such events occurring within an organization presuppose that it has been designed to both permit them, and to reorganize itself around them. With respect to managing leadership, this is a core task of senior management, and a responsibility of management at all levels, to continuously nurture. It will serve as a principal aid in lightening the burden of management's focus on all the details and opportunities in the execution of ongoing operations. In so doing, it will also serve, as leadership is properly acknowledged to do, to have a multiplicative effect on the efficiency and effectiveness of those operations. How might management help inculcate this?

Communicating

Communications is one of most sensitive topics with respect to organizational design. This is because of its influence on control. If knowledge is power, then power belongs to those who control knowledge. They are those who occupy the point where knowledge is concentrated.

One way to look at this subject is to speculate about the uses to which that power might be put, depending on where it is concentrated and controlled. Typically, organizations have been designed to transmit information upward, where it is analyzed. It is then converted into policy and instructions, which are retransmitted downward. The results of the consequent activity generate new information, which is again transmitted upward, continuing the cycle. In such a system, the lateral transmission of information might be viewed as a leak, which compromises the system and reduces the beneficial force of the flow of information through it. First, it might introduce factors and motives that distort the raw accuracy of the information that reaches the top. Second, it could cause what is viewed by the top as premature analysis to occur at lower levels that lack not merely the authority, but also the breadth of perspective necessary to perform that analysis. This could confuse the organization, and disrupt the smooth execution of instructions on their way back down, resulting in increasing degrees of corruption of the system. In this approach, any type of cross-departmental sharing of information that occurs below the top is carefully organized and controlled by the top. Departments rarely communicate directly with each other without the mediation of a higher-level interlocutor.

While this sort of information processing system appears to have a sort of autocratic efficiency about it, it is symptomatic of organizational design thinking that is largely dismissive of its human assets. It views its employees much as it would its material assets, as merely intelligent machinery or data processors. At the very least, it consciously or unconsciously belies the presence of a traditional managerial assumption that the character and capabilities of employees are not naturally consistent with the needs of the organization.

However, it might indicate something else. It may indicate merely that the interests of employees at all levels and those of top management do not coincide. Alternatively, inasmuch as the possession of knowledge equals power, it may turn out to be the case, as well, that those who insist on retaining controlling degrees of it, do so in order to retain power for their benefit, and perhaps not for that of the organization.

We might so conclude because we know that employees have a natural desire to engage in collaborative work enterprises, and that they take important measures of psychological satisfaction from contributing meaningfully to endeavors of larger import than their own individual interests. Well-managed organizations do not merely know this and give lip service to their "most important asset." They organize around it. A workforce that is brought into the organizational ethos takes its aims upon themselves as they operate in its setting. They will, and they want to be given the ability to, contribute in meaningful and individually unique ways to its objectives. In order to do this, they must be given certain degrees of power, and this is done through the provision of information. Armed with this, they can express leadership in the context of the operations of the organization, moving and taking the organization's fate at least partially into their own hands. Information really becomes powerful when it is analyzed and processed, and this, in turn, becomes possible—and, certainly, more potent—when it is widely disseminated, including laterally. So, when such dissemination is precluded from the design of the organization, what are we to conclude?

Perhaps, that top management has made a specific decision to retain control. This would suggest, as well, that they want to arrogate permanently to themselves the expression of all of the proactive efforts and initiatives of the organization. This a common and practical concern that can occur for a variety of reasons. Top management may sincerely believe that only it is capable of managing the organization, and must be aware of, and direct, every significant activity occurring within it. There are times when the urgency of events demands directive managerial methods. Such occasions are rare, and actually do not always call properly for such an approach, but recourse to it is nevertheless frequently and defensibly justified on such grounds. On the other hand, top management may have succumbed to the theories of individual leadership of organizations that are the target of this book. Such theories, while making much of the need to trust and empower subordinates, tend to concentrate the virtues and meaningful capabilities of the organization in those who lead it. Thus, they concentrate in them, as well, power over it.

As mentioned previously, this tends to corrupt the relationship between the organization and its senior executives. Which serves which? Which gives expression to the interests of which? In the context of the present discussion, if the executive at the top is to personally perform so signal and profound a role as that of the individual leader, he will need to have personal and signally profound control over the information contained within the organization. Further, since much theory generated by the modern leadership movement suggests that organizations need to be designed specifically in order to give efficient and effective expression to the inspired leadership of the leader, we may reasonably conclude that their design should dilute neither that leadership nor that organizational expression of it. Which brings us back to controlled vertical transmission of information and instructions, and the limitation and careful monitoring of lateral communication and information processing.

Communication is clearly a key factor in the design of an organization, and an overarching influence on how it thinks, behaves, and operates. The design of an organization can affect how information, instructions, and power are communicated and distributed throughout it, and how flexibly it perceives and adapts to changing circumstances. In fact, in an organization managed with an awareness of the leadership assets it inherently contains, its shape and form can alter in accordance with how that information is communicated and analyzed.

Lateral communication and the authority to act on it are examples of this. In *The Effective Executive*, Peter Drucker describes the modern executive as someone who views his role in the organization from the perspective of how he is able to contribute to its work, or to the work of others attempting to do so. Drucker combines this with his pioneering concept of the *knowledge worker* as being someone who works, not by doing something—by performing a physical action, as on an assembly line, for example—but by providing and inserting knowledge into the value chain of a process. In the past, he says, knowledge workers were largely sole proprietors, such as doctors operating a general practice. Increasingly, however, they are found in organizational settings, and thus are transforming how those organizations look and operate. Properly, knowledge workers look for ways to use their knowledge to contribute to the organization, which gives them important executive characteristics. He cites the modern hospital as a *knowledge organization*, where lateral communication and the authority to act on it result in the self-creation, self-operation, and self-dissolution of teams of professionals from completely different departments and areas of expertise. The unifying element is their joint effort to contribute to the treatment of a patient. The existence, nature, actions, and duration of these teams will vary according to the needs of the patient. The existence of this phenomenon is enabled by an organization that incorporates into the design of its structure its own continual flexible adaptation to the demands placed on it as evaluated, not by its senior executives, but by its operating level employees.

This sort of flexible organization exists in numerous areas, ranging from the film production industry to task-organizing military units. Their uniting feature is that they have designed lateral communication into their organizations in a manner that both distributes and diffuses information, and its processing, throughout the organization. This allows, and even causes, the organization to re-form itself around the results of that information processing activity. The medium in which such remarkable and constructive phenomena occur is the organizational leadership inherent in the organization, which is being intelligently managed as a potent asset by its executives.

EXECUTION

The essential character of an organization may be described as arising from how it is designed, or how it disseminates, processes, and acts on information. These, however, merely assist the organization to pursue its principal aim, which is to accomplish its stated purpose. Having designed the organization, its managers must now use it to perform the activities that will create its intended output. They must use the organization to execute.

Direction

The direction of an organization is a function of its management. Since direction incorporates the idea of initiation, or provision and shaping, of impetus to an action, it is not quite the same as a synonym for management. It is more specific an activity, and thus is subordinate to management, which comprehends and integrates it with all the other activities and processes of the organization.

At the highest levels, direction of the organization arises from, and is an expression of, its strategic management. At operational levels, it is a function of the management of particular endeavors and initiatives engaged in by the organization. At the tactical level, it represents the management of the day-to-day activities of the organization as it pursues its operational objectives. If management should have a bias toward acting at the strategic level, it should also have a bias toward the delegation of all other activities to lower levels in the organization.

In the military, there is a parable of the flagpole used to illustrate this point. A board of senior officers interviewing junior lieutenants for higher assignment calls them in one by one, and presents them each with the same hypothetical task. They are told that they must erect a flagpole. The assets available to them to do so are provided: a detailed list of the material, such as components and construction equipment, and a small team of soldiers to do the work, headed by a sergeant. They are told to explain to the board how they will do it. Each lieutenant, eager to demonstrate his intelligence, planning skills, and ability to think on his feet, hesitates only a moment before describing how he would use the human and material resources provided him, step by detailed step, to accomplish the task. The last lieutenant, however, does not hesitate at all. He tells the board that he would simply turn to the sergeant and say, "Sergeant, build the flagpole." He is the one who wins the assignment.

While we are not told what the lieutenant would be doing in the meanwhile, it is just as well that he is somewhere out of the way while the work is being accomplished. The management technique he has employed is called pushing authority to the lowest possible or practical level. This has the multiple benefits of putting the direction of the task in the hands of he who is most familiar with it and with the resources involved in it, and of leaving the manager to focus on broader tasks more appropriate to his position. Further, note that the sergeant is not told how to do the task, just to do it. He and his team are specifically encouraged to use their own initiative in the endeavor.

Employees in organizations like this are trained in their basic skills, of course. However, they are also trained to expect to be called upon to use their initiative in deploying them. They are taught leadership traits, and they are expected to use them. As a result, they find themselves directing much of the tactical, and even operational, level activities of the organization, releasing their managers to concentrate on longer-term and strategic issues.

Evaluation

Another military caution to commanders is that what you inspect is what your unit does. The lieutenant will have to return from the officer's club, or wherever he has been occupying himself, to ensure that the flagpole has actually been satisfactorily completed, and he will have to do so in time to take any necessary remedial action before the task deadline expires. Further, his doing so will encourage his subordinates to self-inspect. The saying is typically interpreted to mean that your subordinates will do what they know will be checked, and that they may tend to neglect the rest. The caution in this is that much supervision is of issues visible to the supervisor's seniors, which opens the possibility that the unit is focusing its efforts and developing its skills in merely superficial areas. The caution suggests that you should be careful of what you ask for; it may turn out to be all you get.

However, this is not to be taken to mean that managers should inspect everything in order to ensure every task is being properly accomplished. It means that you should use your limited time to the greatest effect, freeing as much of what remains as possible to devote to issues more appropriate to managerial attention. Like the bottling plant manager, those few, core data items that incorporate in simple ways all the necessary and essential information should be chosen. These data items may not provide detailed information about their components, but they should be of a nature that, if they fall within a given range, they indicate that all of those components are satisfactory, as well. It is only when they do not fall within that range that it is appropriate, or necessary, to look closer.

Such an approach will create an environment in which the employees feel able to stretch and contribute. In such an organization, they will tend to find themselves taking responsibility for their individual actions, and of the organization as a whole. Eager to be constructively contributing to an effective and productive enterprise, they will continuously self-evaluate, and evaluate on a unit and group level, as well. In such an organization, public supervision (like the military unit inspection) becomes less of an exercise in critical evaluation, and more of an opportunity to provide positive feedback and affirmation to the organization.

General Erich von Manstein, a brilliant and observant German field commander of World War II, is said to have once remarked that all officers have two characteristics, one each from a pair of opposites. They are all either smart or stupid, and either energetic or lazy. The smart and energetic ones make great staff officers. They work hard and efficiently on everything the commander wants, regardless of its apparent merit or importance. The stupid and lazy ones can be tolerated as basically harmless, but the stupid and energetic ones are an active danger to the army—they must be found out and eliminated root and branch. The most interesting, however, are the smart and lazy ones. They make the best commanders, because they have learned how to prioritize. They know what is important, and refuse to waste their time on what is not. They are not easily confused or startled into pointless action. Rather, they think clearly, and they analyze everything according to its effect on the unit and its ability to accomplish its mission. They are able to efficiently separate the wheat from the chaff, and to avoid expending their, and the organization's, precious resources in unproductive efforts. This is why our lieutenant won the higher assignment.

MONITORING

Aside from the evaluation and supervision of specific tasks and processes, managers need to monitor the interconnective effects of all the organization's endeavors on its overall health and sustainability, as well as its progress toward accomplishment of its goals. Again, important information in this regard is daily obtained by employees at various points in the organization interacting with each other, or with other individuals and organizations external to their own. It is not uncommon for employees at the lowest levels to develop on their own, or to have passed along to them by astute external interlocutors or observers, quite sophisticated assessments of the condition of the organization and the macro-level impacts of its operations. Managers would be well advised to design systems for gathering and evaluating this data. They would also do well to delegate, to the lowest level possible, any action that this data suggests as necessary. It should be quite an ordinary event for those even at the lowest levels of the organization to intervene in tactical level organizational activities, if and as appropriate, in response to tactical level feedback. Simultaneously, information regarding the issue should be gathered and assessed by management for incorporation into preparations for future endeavors.

A key, and perhaps obvious, example of the benefit of such employee initiative would be in efforts designed to continue successful actions, adjust them when environmental feedback so indicates, and to repair or replace them when they conclude that they simply aren't working. Certainly, the soldiers in the front line of an advancing military unit are not expected to wait for higher-level assessments of what they know best themselves, nor for approval to take the appropriate action. They are generally expected to do so on their own authority. Any well-managed organization should examine how effectively it is making use of natural employee leadership initiative in this area.

The central purpose of monitoring the day-to-day activities of an organization is to ensure that problems are identified and addressed in a timely manner. This can hardly be better done than by on-scene employees who are properly trained to identify and deal with common issues, and who are armed with the authority to do so. It is useful for them to be armed, as well, with the authority to act based on their experience, when unforeseen circumstances arise, and their judgment tells them the matter cannot wait.

Maintenance also refers, however, to ensuring the sustainability of discrete operations and of the organization as a whole. Very often, employees have insights, or have them conveyed to them by knowledgeable outsiders, that have sustainability implications in departments or operational levels other than their own. Means should be found to encourage, assess, and respond to concerns or advice about what might otherwise be viewed as managerial-level issues that are raised by non-managerial-level employees or, perhaps, at interference in departmental operations by outsiders. An organization where it is common to hear employee discussions of such issues end with, "Above my pay grade," is risking much. Information that is likely to be of practical—and, perhaps, immediate—value to the organization is being allowed to leak away from it. Further, the natural and constructive instincts of the employees to concern themselves at such a deep level with the organization's welfare will very likely degenerate though neglect. Along with it, the organization will lose numerous productivity enhancing benefits associated with employee-generated organizational leadership.

This area is also connected with closing the loop in the ebb and flow of activities in the organization. Operational cycles repeat, and discrete endeavors come to an end and are replaced by new ones. A well-monitored and maintained unit will use such occasions to assess and rejuvenate all organizational resources, including, of course, its human ones. Employees will have much of value to say in this process. However, this is also a particularly good time to encourage and analyze their input regarding the selection of the next endeavors and the redeployment of organizational assets. While management rarely views this as an appropriate activity, the potential for it to learn and increase its knowledge and effectiveness for the organization is considerable. Furthermore, it is an excellent opportunity to share managerial thinking with the rest of the organization. When such events are conducted with honesty and integrity, they also serve as a mechanism for reinforcing and entrenching the group cohesion that gives rise to organizational leadership. Accordingly, the organization starts anew at all levels.

Peter Drucker also observes, in *The Effective Executive*, that properly managed organizations are dull, boring places. He is referring to the success of such organizations in having developed efficient routines that enable any properly trained employee and manager to deal with day-to-day operations, and to have effectively incorporated into these routines lessons learned from past emergencies or concerns. This enables managers to focus on proper managerial issues, rather than to have their attention drawn repeatedly into crisis management.

On the other hand, the popular image of a dynamic organization headed by a modern, charismatic individual leader is of intense energy emanating from the center, inspiring vibrancy, enthusiasm, and even apparent pandemonium in all directions. Some such leaders actually take pride in the chaos they intentionally cultivate in their staffs, imagining it to be a source of creative energy. Certainly, our business journalist expected something along those lines when he visited a manager referred to him as producing such sterling results in such fundamental areas as consistently superior profits for the bottom line and consistently superior managers for the future sustainability of the organization. However, what he actually saw was an uncluttered office and a manager with what he initially thought was an alarmingly open schedule. This calmness and sobriety reigned at all levels of the plant. It was practically relentless. The organization had structured itself and shaped its communication and operating processes in a manner that developed and employed appropriate strengths and abilities at appropriate levels. The bottling plant was a place where calmness and routine was the rule, rather than crisis and frenzy. Plant management had not only mastered, and made routine, day-to-day operations; it also continuously learned and adapted lessons into those routines. Clearly, the manager was quite smart—and perhaps a little lazy, as well. He certainly knew how to avoid superficial and unnecessary expressions of individual leadership, to cultivate organizational leadership, instead, from within his plant, and to deploy it sustainably and effectively. The business journalist may have found the manager's office to be a disappointingly dull and boring place, but it surely should have served as a nice, quiet sanctum for an inner journey to ponder lessons about how to manage leadership.

PART III
Conclusion

For, impartially speaking,
the French are as much better critics than the English, as they are worse poets.

Thus we generally allow
that they better understand the management of war than our islanders;
but we know we are superior to them
in the day of battle.

They value themselves on their generals,
we on our soldiers.

John Dryden

8

What's Different

"A long habit of not thinking a thing wrong,
gives it a superficial appearance of being right."

—*Thomas Paine*

The terms *leader* & *leadership* have been used for millennia to refer to individuals and how they lead organizations. The suggestion, as some might argue that I have more or less made, that this view has either been an unfortunate and amazingly enduring oversight or, at least, is no longer accurate, is likely to be met with skepticism. Why should we suddenly re-evaluate centuries of thinking that has not only been perfectly adequate to the tasks to which it has been put, but that has helped inspire and mobilize mankind to accomplish some of its greatest achievements? Do the arguments of this book really stand up against the weight of mankind's history with a more familiar notion of leadership?

There are numerous ways that leadership is perceived, sought, and employed. They all offer their own unique, and even powerful, criticisms of the arguments made in this book. Nevertheless, I believe that the concept of organizational leadership will hold up against such counter-arguments. Moreover, I believe that it will emerge from such a debate as a robust and beneficial framework for understanding and managing organizations. The purpose of this chapter, then, is to anticipate and present some of these critiques,[14] and to attempt to answer them. This chapter will try to show why the concept of organizational leadership described in this book is a distinction with an actionable difference.

BUSINESS AS WAR?

The idea of organizational leadership as something that arises naturally from within the organization was inspired, to a large extent, by observations of the military. Further, extensive readings in this area led to the identification of S. L. A. Marshall's description of how many of the front line soldiers he interviewed advanced against enemy fire. While appearing on the face of it to be providing examples of traditional individual leadership, this description actually helped suggest the model of leadership from within the organization that has been argued in this book.

However, military units are organized and trained for combat, and S. L. A. Marshall's observations were specifically of the behavior of such units while under enemy fire. There is hardly any more intense or stressful an environment, and it is difficult to imagine any other organization that could be expected to experience anything even approaching it. How, then, can lessons drawn from such an organization operating in such an environment be applied to distinctly dissimilar organizations that will never operate in that environment?

Take, for example, the observation that, under the stress of combat, many soldiers were unable to perform the most basic duties for which they had been trained, becoming instead merely a core of stoic supporters within the unit. The argument in this book is that such soldiers froze and wound up awaiting, albeit perhaps even giving some sort of moral support or inspiration to, individual exhibitions of heroic leadership by other individuals in the unit. These others engaged in fire and movement, which, after all, was their quite basic job in those circumstances. The stoic supporters then more or less silently moved up alongside these leaders, and the process began again. Even if we can accept this as an intriguing interpretation of events, how can we imagine non-military organizations experiencing them? What sort of stress could a civilian organization undergo that would so paralyze its employees that they simply were rendered psychologically unable to perform basic, routine duties?

The heart of this criticism is that these extreme levels of stress, which gave rise to the behaviors being used to draw generally applicable lessons about organizational behavior, do not occur in other organizations. Thus, the behaviors won't, either, and the lessons drawn from them will not apply.

The behaviors observed, however, were actually of varying levels of motivation, as well as of stress, and of the effects of their interaction on the organization and its individuals. Stress will occur, or be experienced, at varying levels by individuals in any organization. Their basic organizational morale will also exist at different levels, and be affected to different degrees, according to the stress felt from any source by them and the organization as a collective whole.

The high degrees of stress and extremes of morale observed within the military do not mean that military units operate in an organizational sphere distinct from that in which civilian organizations operate. Neither does it mean that the fundamental principles of organizational psychology operate in wholly different ways in the military than out of it. Rather, they operate in the same universe, ordered according to the same unifying principles. If a military combat unit and the staff of a public library seem to come from entirely different worlds, we must discipline ourselves to see that they are really living at, perhaps, opposite poles of the same spectrum. This spectrum is composed of the nature and degrees of intensity of the interplay of the principals of organizational psychology that influence or underlie the behavior of all organizations. Any staff, engaged in any activity, can become demoralized and passive. On the other hand, any staff can become inspired and proactive. However, the forces that give rise to these organizational conditions are likely to stand out more starkly at the intensive end of the spectrum. Thus, the relations between the underlying factors and those conditions may be more easily discerned, and their lessons may be more easily drawn and described, at that end of the spectrum.

That said, the degrees of pressure and stress that can be generated in non-military enterprises should not be understated. Frequently, civilian organizations feel the need to undertake new endeavors, or are met with competition or threats to their viability from unexpected quarters, that throw them into quite desperate struggles. Often, these struggles are costly in both material and human terms, and may even call into question the ability of the organization to survive. Whether gambling all on a new market or product, risking organizational integrity in a merger or acquisition, or fighting to recover lost ground to a competitor who has stolen a technological march, organizations and all of their members can experience quite high levels of stress. Just as in the military, anticipation of such events can be as, or more, daunting than the events themselves. Considering or dealing with the possibility of failure, and the consequent destruction to reputations or careers, can be devastating. It can be very stressful, even in a civilian enterprise, to undertake an endeavor knowing that one's ability to support one's self and one's family may be jeopardized, or that one's actions will potentially jeopardize the ability of others to support themselves and their families. This can initiate the types of dynamics in any organization that result in the sorts of behavior observed by S. L. A. Marshall in combat units.

Furthermore, the phenomenon of a core of stoic supporters generating and adapting to expressions of leadership by other individuals does not require high degrees of organizational stress to occur. It can arise from any of a number of private abilities, skills, motivations, or other concerns that individuals bring with them into the organizational setting, combined with the degree to which managers are aware of, or successful in managing, the organizational leadership environment in the organization. It is quite common, both in quiescent and in dynamic periods of an organization's life, to find a large number of employees who seem to be hanging back or riding the coattails of the hard work and initiative of others. Yet, in either situation, these phenomena can be equally indicative of an influential and positive organizational leadership environment, or can point to the potential for cultivating one.

The differences between military and non-military organizations can indeed be sufficiently large to warrant caution when drawing comparisons between them. Many of these cautions were offered at the opening to Chapter 4. As indicated there, however, the area of greatest concern is in the comparison of the character and functions of individual leaders at the head of combat units, with those at the head of non-military organizations. Even there, much can be learned. However, the process should be engaged in with care in order to avoid drawing unwarranted parallels. Nevertheless, the military organization itself, as a setting for the accomplishment of large aims by individuals brought together for that purpose, operates within the same set of rules governing organizational behavior anywhere. Indeed, many of those rules were discovered, and the lessons drawn from them were applied in the civilian world, by military personnel or students of the military, particularly after the mass demobilization following World War II. Business is not war. Nevertheless, individuals engaged collectively in organizational activities behave and are affected by events in similar ways whatever may be those activities.

GREAT MEN

Much debate, particularly among historians, has revolved around the presumed phenomenon of Great Men in war, politics, science, the arts, and other fields. The question is concerned with whether such individuals actually perpetrate a singular change in the course of events in the history of their area. In other words, can history be made the tool of Great Men, or are they merely the unwitting tools of history?

Many argue that the extraordinary achievements of men such as Alexander the Great, Julius Caesar, or Napoleon, to take just three, unleashed events that changed the flow of history forever and in irreproducibly unique ways. Alexander's conquests unified and Hellenized the Greater Middle East, with consequences for subsequent events that were of immediate import for centuries, and that are arguably still felt today. The diversion of Republican Rome to empire by the conqueror of Europe had still more direct influence on everything from the ambitions of subsequent conquering nations to modern visions of the European identity. Napoleon's exploits helped unleash on the world the multiple effects of the French Revolution, such as nationalism and the modern European concept of citizenship.

Many others, however, argue that Great Men are simply the human faces of historical trends already underway. This argument would have it that these individuals, while certainly of remarkable personal ability and character, are basically plucked from the masses by the interplay of larger events in order to act out the roles thrust upon them by history, and to facilitate the expression of history's intent. According to this view, Alexander's conquests would likely have been accomplished in some fashion, by someone, at some point in time. He lived in an age of warrior princes whose whole art of statecraft was to wage war and conquer new territory. Several hundred years later, Julius Caesar is said to have regretted that he had not managed to equal the conquests of Alexander by the same age. Just as was Caesar, Napoleon, too, was inspired to exceed the conquests of his predecessors. Many of the expressions and effects of the French Revolution transpired in spite of Napoleon's instincts, rather than because of him. While such men were conscious of their place in history, their ambitions must be said to have been largely personal, and their accomplishments remarkable events that would likely have been attained by some one or another, anyway, of the multitude of princes engaged in this effort. It can be difficult to argue that their careers represented conscious efforts to shape and influence history according to some grand, transforming view of the future.

Does this book take the side of those supporting the idea that there are no Great Men, that the forces of history are dominant? Actually, no. There are many others who I feel must be regarded as Great Men who consciously worked to redirect the flow of history according to a vision of the future, with the result that they exhibited a large measure of personal influence on that subsequent history. These men carried large numbers of their contemporaries with them along in their visions, and created great, enduring, and dynamic movements. Among such Great Men can be counted the Founding Fathers of the United States of America. Many argue that history was flowing in their direction anyway. To date, however, the forces of history have not produced another country like the United States, with its unique culture of personal sovereignty and responsibility, and its singularly conscious role in, and influence upon, history itself. The argument that such a culture was the inevitable result of the sort of people who took political and religious refuge in a presumably new land also lacks persuasiveness. Such colonies were established throughout the Americas, and even elsewhere in the world, with somewhat more traditional historical results. Perhaps the flow of the undercurrents of history made such men as the Founding Fathers possible, but it did not make their accomplishments inevitable.

So, what does this say about the argument of this book that the heads of organizations should merely manage them, rather than follow the examples provided by such Great Men, and aspire to provide to their organizations, employees, and communities similarly inspirational, far-seeing, and influential leadership? Well, the reason is that most who attempt to follow the Great Man model of leadership find themselves in imitation of Alexander and not Washington, Caesar and not Jefferson, Napoleon and not Hamilton. The modern model of individual leadership tends to psychically separate those leaders from their organizations, train the focus of attention on their personal aspirations and ambitions, and transform their organizations into merely the vehicles for attaining them. Even those who aspire to accomplishments in the style of the Founding Fathers displace the value of those accomplishments from their purpose to the reputation of the person who accomplished them. Washington did not do what he did to set any new records—to compete with Caesar or Alexander. He did it to bring a new nation into being that might beneficially alter the course of history. Many students of the modern leadership movement, however, are more interested in establishing an individual reputation for great leadership than in securing the future of their organizations.

Furthermore, while much is made of the supposedly paradigm-shifting winds of change presently sweeping the world, most organizations do not really contend with conditions that call for such leadership. While creating a new course for the river of history may be a remarkable achievement, it is also perilous. The creativity and energy arising from such fundamental efforts are usually generated from the destruction they cause. It is best that such undertakings be thrust upon us by history, rather than foisted upon us by our presumed leaders.

GREAT INNOVATORS

The forgoing notwithstanding, it might still be argued that the great innovators of the past, if not its Great Men, exhibited an influential and exemplary form of individual leadership that can properly be pursued by heads of organizations, today. Some established important new industries, such as John D. Rockefeller, who created the first great oil enterprise, or Thomas Watson who turned IBM into the first major computer company and an enduring standard for the industry. Others created or pioneered new techniques of revolutionary import, such as Henry Ford's assembly line production process, George Gallup's statistical public opinion research methods, or the concept of retailing through chain stores developed by George Huntington and George Gilman. Surely, such innovations created new ways of producing and distributing wealth, as well as of channeling human ingenuity and energy for the benefit of all, and their pursuit as an individual endeavor is to be encouraged.

Many of the innovations that have left their mark on the way people live today were made in fields such as science and the arts. Here, much, if not most, innovative activity has historically been conducted by individuals. Artistic, literary, and musical insights and advances have been made by single virtuosos, writers, or composers. The great scientific discoveries and inventions in the past have been made by great minds working in small laboratories, either alone, or with the assistance of student apprentices. Actually, much research is still conducted this way. In this context, there is little organizational relevance to their activities. On those occasions when they are followed by larger enterprises based on the original innovation, the individual nature of the innovative process is not diluted by its subsequent organizational expression, nor is the management of the organization necessarily an expression of that innovation—merely a commercial or other consequence of it. Today, on the other hand, much scientific research is conducted by larger organizations. In this case, the operations of the individual innovation and organizational management process might appear to have become commingled. However, they, in fact, are not. Scientific innovation remains a function of insight and inspiration on an essentially individual level, however large the research teams, or how collaborative the chief research scientists, might be. Their work represents fundamentally individual—not organizational—activity; regardless of the setting in which it occurs. The organization's contribution is to provide the facilities, and to cultivate the environment for such innovation to occur. However, the organization itself is neither managed by something called "innovation," nor by someone who routinely does it.

A good example of this is the legendary 3M system of permitting employees to spend a portion of their time on exploring new ideas or inventions of personal interest to them. This has made 3M famous for innovation and the development of cutting edge products. However, it cannot really be said that 3M is operated by innovative leadership. When an employee makes a discovery or innovation that may be commercially feasible, the next step is to convince an influential member of management of that. If successful, that manager then mentors the employee through the process of developing a comprehensive brief regarding the commercial prospects of the innovation, and the appropriateness of its pursuit by 3M. This brief, together with those by other employees who have made their own unique discoveries, is presented by the employee to a board of senior managers. These assess the proposed projects and determine which, if any, meet the feasibility threshold. Then, they select those to which they are willing to devote limited corporate resources. This is not innovative leadership. It is a combination of intelligent management of organizational leadership as expressed through individual insight and innovation, and of a hard-nosed assessment and decision-making process. That is to say, it is effective management.

The great innovators of the business world, such as those mentioned in the first paragraph of this section, may seem to be in a different category. Since they headed large enterprises, and their innovations involved the creation of new types of endeavors or new ways of operating them, perhaps they represent a proper model of innovative individual leadership of organizations. On closer examination, however, we can see that they really were engaged principally in managing their organizations, not in leading them through a process of innovative leadership. They sought and discovered new resources, or techniques of mobilizing and deploying old ones, to more effectively and efficiently serve the purpose of the organization. There was much value to attaining the degrees of economic integration, scale, and influence that Rockefeller achieved. Ford pioneered a production process that, however innovative, was essentially a new management technique, not a method of leadership. Gallup's techniques for public opinion research are highly influential and effective tools that have shown themselves to be of benefit in a number of areas to organizations of many types. However, the innovation they represent amounts largely to a personal scientific one; it is merely given commercial expression organizationally. And the concept of chain-store retailing invented in its modern form by Huntington and Gilman is also basically a management technique that enables a company's retailing efforts to be extended to such a large market as to increase its purchasing power, and give it economies of scale in current operations.

Thus, innovative leadership is not really a viable leadership approach for heads of organizations. A principal duty of such senior executives is to manage as efficiently as possible. If, in so doing, they hit upon what turns out to be an innovative management technique, it remains a management technique. It cannot be transformed into a durable leadership technique which itself is characterized principally by innovation, or by preemptive and proactive change. While it may be dull, it is an unavoidable fact that organizations are created to accomplish their chartered purposes, not to exhibit change. It is worth noting, as well, that the business innovators noted above all owned their enterprises at the time that they implemented their innovations. If a modern contracted manager wants to emulate their innovativeness as a matter of leadership technique, he would best emulate their ownership position as well.

The topic of innovative leadership brings into the subject another example of why it is often difficult to keep discussions of this general theme on track. The term *leader* is a very plastic word that has a wide range of applications. It is routinely used to refer generally, rather than in a technical sense, to those who head enterprises. That is, anyone who is in charge of anything, from a temporary task force to a major organization, is usually referred to as a *leader*. This is commonly meant to convey his position of responsibility or authority as the head of the group. It does not normally or necessarily convey the more or less technical meaning of a *leader* as an individual who consciously expects himself to personally exhibit all the leadership functions of an organization. As we have seen, various and sundry divisions of the modern leadership movement simultaneously promote a quite wide number of differing, and often mutually irreconcilable, definitions of what a leader is. This phenomenon is, itself, evidence of the fact that such definitions are not generally or intimately associated with the ordinary daily use of the word.

Consequently, it should be noted that it is difficult to get around using the word *leader* in the normal course of a discussion of a senior executive, even when, as I do, one wishes to stress the executive's role as a manager and not a leader. It is too common, ordinary, and useful a term to be avoided. The result is recourse to inelegant circumlocutions in an effort to distinguish between the general, broad understanding of the word, and the wide swath of specific technical definitions proposed for it by the modern leadership movement. It bears pointing out, then, that there will be many instances where an individual is appropriately referred to as a leader in the general sense, without it following therefrom that he is assuming the quasi-technical characteristics of the term that are the causes of concern giving rise to this book.

OPEN SCHEDULES

Is there nothing at all, then, for senior management to do in the area of leadership? Is it only left to them to simply manage the leadership originating from lower in the organization, and then to defer to it?

First, deference commonly implies the superiority of that to which one defers. There are certain cultural mores, for example, that call for deference to elders in acknowledgment of their superior accumulated wisdom and experience. However, this is both non-organizational in nature, is itself limited, and has important reciprocal elements. The real concern here, however, is about the apparent abrogation of managerial authority and responsibility by yielding to "superior" expressions of leadership from below.

In ordinary organizational situations, it is not always necessary or appropriate to generalize this connotation from particular instances to ordinary practice. For instance, in matters of medicine we typically defer to those with superior training in that field. Even though our responsibility for our own health is greater than that of whatever doctor may be treating us at any given time, we will likely acknowledge the doctor's superior knowledge and accede to his advice. Similarly, in a business meeting where the feasibility of proposed projects is being evaluated, the VP of finance who supports a project based on the cash flow projections briefed for it, may defer to the VP of marketing who casts doubt on the achievability of those forecasts, or to a specialist consultant who questions the viability of the technology involved. In these cases, the deference arises from the acknowledgment of the general superiority of knowledge, experience, or authority of the person deferred to in the area of the matter under discussion.

On the other hand, if the same group is brainstorming ideas for a wholly new enterprise, the VP of operations, despite his own generally superior knowledge, experience, and earned authority in this area, may defer to an idea proposed by a junior, or by someone from another department, if he recognizes it to be a valuable new insight or concept—even if only an inadvertent one. In this case, his general superiority in the area has not generated the superior idea—but it has recognized it, and he has had the sense to adopt it. In other words, he is not yielding his authority or responsibility in a general sense to a source of superior value. Rather, he is using them, in a discrete instance, to recognize and support a good idea. The superiority, in this case, is in he who consciously uses his position to identify and cultivate a beneficial concept, whatever its source. The superior party, here, is the deferrer, rather than the person or thing deferred to.

Even the more general cases of deference to one whose education or training confers expert status can be seen to be more carefully delimited than commonly thought. For example, while we typically defer to doctors, we only do so in the area of medicine, and doing so hardly is viewed as negligent disregard for our responsibility for our own health—rather the reverse. What's more, recent events have led to the leveling of the relationship between laymen and experts, such as medical doctors, requiring the latter to develop the ability to explain and justify their advice. In the business environment, rather than an authority-sapping deference, it is an obvious exercise of responsibility to yield the floor to experts in other areas, even those junior in rank, regarding topics in those other areas.

The accurate way to look at this is to see management and leadership in their proper relationship. Management is superior to leadership, as are managers to leaders. Managers who cultivate leadership as an asset, and who deploy expressions of it by their employees, are managing and using it—not deferring to it. They are exercising their authority, not abrogating it.

Furthermore, the contention in this book is that leadership is a natural and inherent characteristic of any well-managed organization. It is experienced collectively, and expressed individually, throughout the organization and all of its members—including management. Individual expressions of leadership are manifested according to the skills, training, perspective, and locations in place and time of individuals in the organization, and in its interactions with its environment. Managers are influenced by all of these factors, and in organizations characterized by solid group cohesion and a pervasive leadership environment, they will certainly find themselves contributing important instances of it. Among their unique managerial functions is to separate the instance of leadership from the leader, and to recognize the value of the contribution rather than the contributor. This is not to say that any employee, including a manager, who exhibits leadership, is not valuable. It is to say that the phenomenon of leadership is not ineluctably a characteristic of the individual who exhibits any form of it at any given time—it is a characteristic of the organization itself.

Managers are intimately involved in the leadership of their organizations. Certainly, they will sometimes find themselves expressing that leadership as individuals, just as do others in the organization. However, they will always be occupied in managing both this valuable organizational asset, and the expression of it by all the organization's members.

ALL IN THE WRIST?

It is possible that there are those who have been persuaded to stipulate to the conclusions argued in this book, but who then go further and express concerns that there remains an unwarranted focus on leadership in the organization. If an untoward focus on the special character, privileges, and contributions of leadership as expressed in the senior executive is likely to produce counterproductive results for both him and the organization, won't an untoward focus on his unique duty to manage it do the same? Does he not now become a kind of honored, wizened steward of a rare and precious strand of human nature? In fact, doesn't this special obligation place an even greater charge on him to become the organization's supreme expert on the topic, so that he can better manage it? And what about the organization itself? Is it supposed to become some sort of peculiar incubator, where people just mill around like a flock of Great Men, until they begin to spontaneously combust with random, enigmatic flashes of leadership, which the managers are supposed to capture, make sense of, and harness for use?

Managing leadership is not some special trick or insight for making management's problems go away. It is not a secret technique that will make one manager rise above his benighted peers. The apparent focus on leadership is in fact apparent, and merely a function of the topic of this book. I do not suggest that managers can simply put the right ingredients in the organizational pot, stir it until they have created just the right mixture at just the right temperature so that organizational leadership begins to rise like steam from the brew, powering all the leadership functions, and then just try to remember to return occasionally to stir the pot again.

Leadership is merely one of many assets of the organization. They all require professional and expert attention to identify, cultivate, and deploy in a comprehensive, concerted, and sustainable fashion for the benefit of the organization. Some of these assets are tangible, such as raw materials. Some are consumed during the organization's operations, and some depreciate over longer periods. Some are internal to the organization and under its control. Others are external and merely potential, or "volunteer," assets. Their service as assets only even exists to the extent to which the organization recognizes their availability and successfully marshals them in its cause. Still others are intangible, but no less vital, contributors to the successful operations of the enterprise. Organizational leadership is one of these, just one of many—but one that if intelligently managed, is capable of aiding in the management of the others.

Senior management has too much to do to become obsessed with the presumably exalted qualities of leadership, whether they reside in an individual or the organization as a whole. Appointing a VP of Organizational Leadership, like similar offices of Learning or Knowledge, is entirely unnecessary, and would not be the least bit productive. The latter offices are engaged in a traditional task, the management of the acquisition and productive diffusion of information and knowledge in an organization. They may, perhaps, be justified as separate staff departments because the promises and demands of technology are driving these functions to be performed at unprecedented levels of sophistication and efficiency. The management of organizational leadership, on the other hand, requires little more than knowing that it needs to be done, and then doing it. All that managers need to do is to come to an understanding of leadership as a feature inherent in the organization that has the potential to function as an asset. This calls for shifts in the ways managers approach personnel management and organizational culture, but these are not of the order of magnitude that require whole new layers of bureaucracy or administration.

The organization and its employees continue about their normal business. They meet, plan, produce, and interact with vendors, customers, competitors, and peers. A main feature of the notion of organizational leadership is simply that the cohesion that binds them to each other in the organizational setting is valued, and is awarded managerial attention. Next, they learn that their sense of general responsibility for the organization as a whole and its members is respected, cultivated, and drawn upon by management. They neither avoid, nor does management chasten them for, making efforts that they might otherwise have the inclination and ability to make, just because they are "above my pay grade." Employee activity and behavior does not change in remarkable ways. It just begins to emerge from, or center itself on—rather than be firmly bounded by—specific jobs and functions.

PILING ON

Placing the execution of the leadership functions of an organization in the hands of its employees sounds like quite an extraordinary thing to do. While the concept of organizational leadership might seem to make sense on a theoretical level, it actually seems quite risky and counterintuitive to take the control of the organization away from its senior executives, who we always thought were its leaders, and give it to their juniors. Maybe there is really something else going on here. Is this really just another trick for getting greater productivity out of increasingly downsized, overburdened, and demoralized work forces? Is characterizing organizational leadership as a function expressed by the employees actually some sort of clever ploy to flatter them and humble management, encouraging the employees to accept the Trojan Horse, which only then opens to release the additional obligations that further oppress them?

The idea of organizational leadership begins with the apparently ennobling idea of employees being not only able, but also often better suited than management, to perform the leadership functions of the organization. It then goes on to promote the idea of the management of that leadership phenomenon in the organization, just like any other of its assets. This could well be characterized as stark manipulation. The whole process might seem to be an exercise in cynicism. However, the concepts are neither as ennobling nor as manipulative as all that, and they certainly are not cynical.

The history of collaborative enterprise has been characterized by the increasingly constructive and productive involvement of the labor force in organizations. Particularly in the 20th century, students of organizational behavior began to understand that labor had much more to offer to the value adding process of production than the mere operation of machines and movement of material. Management has noted these lessons and learned to apply them to the benefit of all concerned, including the employees. It is pointless and impractical to suggest that efforts to improve the condition of employees, in order to make them more productive, simply represent crass manipulation. Certainly, the alternative is not to return to the age when management neither "manipulated" the working conditions or morale of employees, nor paid these any mind at all. Just as certainly, the alternative is not to suppose that organizations should take on the moral and material welfare of their employees as equal or superior duties to their chartered purposes.

Organizations are created to accomplish specified aims, and their members are mobilized and managed to that end. No involved party has any real misapprehensions about this. On the contrary, adults typically have a psychologically healthy and mature desire to contribute to enterprises that encompass greater purposes than those bound by their private lives. Employment in an organization offers the opportunity to combine physical and psychological maintenance needs in increasingly satisfying ways as employees and management both learn more about their organizations. Drawing the greatest possible value from the available efforts and abilities of both employees and management produces ever-growing benefits for all concerned. Far from serving as a fig leaf for cynical exploitation of the one by the other, it increasingly represents the enlightened and intelligent identification and alignment of their interests.

SILVER STAKE

If employees are increasingly involved in the operations of their organizations, even the planning of them, then are they not increasing their ownership of them as well? After all, there is a burgeoning movement among critics that all those who are affected by an organization must be viewed as having a stake in what it does. Deriving from this, they argue, is their right to also have a say. Isn't the idea of organizational leadership, existing and emanating from the individuals within the organization, another development along these lines? It seems, after all, to promote the idea that employees ought to be given a greater sense of involvement and responsibility for the organization and each other. It even seems that they are being given control over some of the planning and operational functions traditionally associated strictly with management. Does this mean that they are to be given a greater say in the decision-making process as well? In fact, if they are being given greater responsibility, how can they not be given the commensurate scope to express it?

To say that one has a stake in someone else's actions is to indicate a more or less direct correlation in welfare between the two. The concept comes from the idea of ownership. A stake is a measure of investment risked in an enterprise. An owner clearly is affected by how the organization does. Just as clearly, customers, vendors, employees, and the community at large are affected by the organization. So, the expression that they have a stake is used with them as well. This is then leveraged into an assertion for their being given a say in its operations. There is considerable pressure in various guises for this concept to be given meaningful application. Some management consultancies even promote a wider range of participation in the decision-making process, particularly regarding issues of wide import.

This is precisely the wrong approach for the wrong reason. To begin with, the only parties with the fundamental authority to make decisions for an organization are its owners. This authority is frequently delegated to a board of directors, which further delegates it to professional management. However, this delegated authority is not fundamental. It is merely derived, and its exercise by the delegatees calls for their assumption of a unique managerial obligation called fiduciary responsibility. Employees do not have, and typically cannot be burdened with, this responsibility. Thus, they have neither the ownership right nor the fiduciary responsibility to demand, or be required, to participate in the decision-making process. Any diffusion of fundamentally owner-level rights or responsibilities to parties that do not possess them, nor have been specifically contractually delegated them, represents a dilution of the fiduciary, legal, and ethical foundations of the operation of the enterprise. The employee stake in the enterprise is figurative only, and cannot legitimately be used as the authority to confer on them concrete ownership-level, or even managerial, benefits or privileges.

The existence and functioning of organizational leadership among the employees is not a gift or entitlement given to them. It is not a mechanism provided for employee self-fulfillment, nor is it a quid pro quo for empowering them, and for excusing management of its proper duties or responsibilities. It, simply, is a phenomenon that arises naturally from within organizations, operating with varying degrees of coherence and effectiveness. It can be identified, understood, marshaled, and deployed to the benefit of the organization and all of its members. But management is not relieved of any privileges or obligations, nor do any of these accrue to employees, because the source of leadership has been identified as emanating from within, rather than from atop, the organization.

Management retains the hard job of setting priorities and making decisions. There is no avoiding or diluting that. Taking advantage of organizational leadership simply extends the reach and effectiveness of the leadership functions. The taking by employees of action as, itself, an expression of leadership or judgment is typically done at the tactical level of the organization's activities. Even then, it is understood to be executed from an authority of derived, delegated, and limited character. This does not mean that the employee needs to look over his shoulder, or that his freedom of tactical movement for the benefit of the organization needs to be carefully or tightly bounded. It only means that management needs to accept and retain responsibility. In the intelligent management of leadership, retention of responsibility means taking it on the chin, without complaint, when an employee effort does not work out. Such instances, barring the most extraordinary circumstances, are not to be responded to with punishment, nor even with restraint, but with enthusiastic support, and collaboration in learning from the experience. In the management of organizational leadership, the general principle is that success is delegated; failure is retained. Managers make sure that credit for accomplishments is firmly awarded to the source, and they just as firmly let their seniors know that responsibility and censure for falling short go no further down into the ranks than the manager, himself.

This is properly viewed neither as manipulative nor as patronizing. Employees are not given ownership rights or fiduciary responsibility for the decision-making processes or operations of the organization, not because they are not capable of bearing them, but because they cannot be given away. Employee participation is an input upon which only management, not the employees, ethically can act. As management cultivates, encourages, and attempts to make productive use of employee expression of organizational leadership for the benefit of all, it is giving all the organization's members a vehicle to influence, but not the right to control or direct, the organization's operations.

NOTHING NEW UNDER THE SUN?

This is all very well and good, but why have we not heard of it before? How is it possible that such a grand and useful idea, capable of relieving the tremendous pressures on senior executives at the same time that it enhances their effectiveness, has not been observed and remarked until now?

Actually, it has. We just have not paid sufficient attention. Observers have contended against the posturing drama of charismatic individual leadership for centuries, even millennia. In the 20th century, writers such as Follett have hinted, sometimes quite broadly, at the existence of self-leadership or self-management phenomena in organizations. However, in a world of high stakes and momentous events, it seems counter-intuitively passive to yield so much control to the organization itself. The last century began with the world accommodating itself to such previously inconceivable endeavors as whole nations mobilizing for war and huge business enterprises girdling the globe. In this environment of political, military, and commercial titans, Follett's ideas about self-organizing and evolving groups may have seemed a little utopian. The second half of the century was ushered in by an epic armed struggle, from which emerged two superpowers, with irreconcilably conflicting worldviews, gripped in a dangerous contest for supremacy that shaped virtually the entire character of the period. Such a mortal rivalry seemed to call for the sounding of certain trumpets by leaders firmly ensconced at the head of their organizations. As the century came to a close, we appeared to be whipsawed by bewildering winds of political, technological, and commercial changes that seemed to demand the firm guidance of visionary leadership from the top.

Nevertheless, all the while, there were voices, some prominent and influential, suggesting that we might have it wrong. Unfortunately, the influence these thinkers did hold tended to arise from aspects of their work unrelated to leadership, or from narrow and specific applications of that work. The ancient and seductive concept of the charismatic individual leader at the top was embellished and enthusiastically marketed by the modern leadership movement. It was just as enthusiastically accepted by those who aspired to exercise its force—or to be rescued by its vision.

We are still feeling the results of the collapse of this fundamentally untenable framework, and we continue, as well, to see additional instances of it emerge. I do not argue that the concept of organizational leadership has never been hinted at before. I do respectfully propose that it is well past time to take a closer look at it. In the concluding chapter, we will examine various avenues for doing that.

9

What's Next

"If a rhinoceros were to enter this restaurant now,
there is no denying he would have great power here.
But I should be the first to rise and assure him
that he had no authority whatever."

—G. K. Chesterton

Placing undue expectations in the persons of individual organizational lead-ers—especially, but not exclusively, in the business field—has led to great disap-pointments. Investing too much faith in the character, ability, and vision of chief executives has contributed to an unfortunate dissolution of the natural and neces-sary bonds between organizations, their executives, their owners, and the larger community. All of these, as well as suppliers, distributors, customers, and credi-tors, have fallen prey to the modern leadership movement's ascription of special and rare qualities to their protégés. We have found to our dismay that they have generally proven to be unequal to the expectations made of them. We and they together have fallen victim to the exaggerated claims about their lofty abilities, only to find together that their ambitions, and thus ours, have been held aloft by exemplars who—while, perhaps, of heroic mien—have feet of clay.

Years of celebration of modern-day leaders at the helm of great "learning" and ever-changing organizations, followed by visions of these same leaders appearing on television talk shows with their lawyers by their sides, or on the news surren-dering to authorities, has been a shock. Even more so, we have seen some great and presumably venerable companies, having virtually attained status as institu-tions of our culture, simply disappear. Even whole industries have been desper-ately shaken by the bursting of, not just the economic bubble, but of the leadership bubble as well.

Our response, unfortunately, has been inadequate. We have sought justice, of course, and perhaps with refreshingly unaccustomed vigor. We have made efforts to legislate accountability into the system by placing additional personal expectations on individual leaders, accompanied by substantial sanctions if they are not met. We have debated the issue of how all the checks and balances failed to catch the excesses and mismanagement with which some of these organizations were apparently riddled.

We have not, however, analyzed with sufficient vigor the underlying assumptions we use to manage our organizations. Our response has been to chasten, threaten, and increase the expectations and pressure we place on the individuals leading them. We have not considered the possibility that it is our very expectation that they lead—rather than manage—that might be at the heart of the problem.

Further, we have insufficiently examined our own culpability. All of us—whether employees or creditors, boards or vendors, the press or the community at large—bought in to the explanation sold us of what a modern organizational leader is, and what our obligations to him are. We accepted on faith the hype about these presumed leaders, and adopted, ourselves, the enthusiasm with which it was presented. Many of us accepted uncritically their vision. We even took our inability to understand that vision as evidence of their possession of the advertised superior abilities, and as confirmation that our proper role was to do or die, and not to question why. Creditors lent vast sums without adequate due diligence. Boards confused their roles, and were persuaded, or co-opted, into supporting the leader, instead of guiding and exercising oversight over him.

Today, various members of the leadership movement actually use many of these disasters as case studies to support their particular approaches to the topic. However, the fact is that any ascription of leadership exclusively or specially to the individual at the top, and in particular to the unique qualities of that individual, is a powerful contribution to the problem. It places unbearable burdens on his self-image and character. It inevitably imposes on all associated parties, be they owners, employers, or other businesses in the value chain, the role of supporters, facilitators, enhancers, and expressers of that singular leadership. This is accompanied by a suppression of appropriate questioning, oversight, and due diligence.

This would suggest that there is more to do than merely the same old thing, only harder. Instead, it is time to have another look at the necessary roles to be played by all the related institutions involved in the activities of organizations.

The concept of leadership itself should be reexamined and exposed to a thorough debate. We need to make sure we have it right.

In this chapter, we will briefly summarize the basic ideas underlying the concept of organizational leadership and its management, as expressed in this book. We will review what it is, and its effects on and benefits for the various key elements of the organization. We will conduct a brief overview of actions that can be taken to implement and institutionalize organizational leadership. We will then conclude with a discussion of what should come next.

ORGANIZATIONAL LEADERSHIP

As we have seen, it can sometimes be difficult to get a grasp on what, exactly, is being discussed, when the topic of the conversation is leadership. The term is broad, elastic, and easily used in a wide variety of settings. It can refer to the status of someone or something in relation to peers, such as a scientific leader, or a market leader. This use does not refer to an individual's characteristics, or to a technique of leadership; it describes who is ahead in a race. On the other hand, it can refer in a generic way to someone in charge of a group. When used this way, the meaning is general. It is a synonym for "boss," head," "supervisor," or for any other word that describes the person in charge. It simply points to who is at the top of the organization; it does not imply any particular overarching expectations to be made of that person.

However, our concern, here, has been with leadership within organizations. It seems pretty clear that leadership occurs in collaborative enterprises, and that individuals respond to it in ways that meaningfully affect the enterprise's ability to accomplish its goals. In fact, leadership does not just haphazardly occur—it can be generated and directed to promote the ends of the organization. For millennia, ways have been sought to learn how to effectively do that. For the most part, however, that search has pointed more or less uniformly in a different direction than that promoted by this book. Why is that?

Missteps

For the better part of human history, the discussion of leadership has had no real meaning except in the context of political struggle. *Leadership* referred to those at the heads of political entities, and their leadership was typically exhibited through military adventure, and the acquisition of power to enable increased freedom of political movement. Moreover, these political entities were generally directly identified with their leaders. In fact, they were equivalent to their leaders. Typically, the leader *was* the state. Very rarely, indeed, was a successful state little more than Emerson's "lengthened shadow of one man." Even Republican Rome became Imperial Rome, at last. And who remembers any of its leaders prior to its first Emperor—and destroyer of the Republic—Julius Caesar?[15]

As a result, the habit of history accustomed us to viewing leadership as something belonging to, and exhibited exclusively by, a single individual at the head of the enterprise. Further, much of the activity of leadership was conducted in the context of political struggle for power and expansion, particularly through warfare. Accordingly, we have developed the practice of examining political, and especially military, history for examples of leadership for us to follow in the conduct of leadership in our modern organizations.

The examples of political leadership we learn from the likes of Plutarch and Machiavelli describe, essentially, the jostling of individuals for self-aggrandizing power. These, one is to hope, have little legitimate application in the modern organizational world. Moreover, as discussed in the beginning of Chapter 4, the lessons of individual leadership taken from the military are frequently inappropriate for direct employment in non-military circumstances.

Nevertheless, the events of the 20th century—from the epochal world wars of its first half, through the bipolar global struggle that characterized its second half, to the uncertain times into which its close seems to have ushered us—have conspired to refocus our efforts, and to invest our hopes, in the effort to discover the secrets of visionary individual leadership. In turn, this, in the last decades of that century, gave rise to the modern leadership movement. This movement has spawned a wide and incoherent array of approaches to the subject. However, they share some noteworthy features. First, they all revolve around the presumed exceptional qualities of individuals who are set up as the superordinate leaders of our organizations. Second, they have a rather strong tendency to see the organization's role as that of giving expression to the leader's leadership. Third, with the application of that rather premodern leadership feature in the modern context, the actual owners of modern organizations, or their representatives, often get wrapped up in the grouping of organizational entities that are described by the leadership movement as beholden to the leader. Fourth, as a result of this, the integrity of the relationship between the key organizational elements of owner, manager, and employee is dangerously weakened, or even impaired altogether. Fifth, the movement's growth appears to have peaked with the popping of the leadership bubble, as represented by the whirlwind of scandal, bankruptcy, and failure that has swept many of our organizations in all fields.

Half Steps

Nevertheless, there have been several voices in the literature that have attempted to throw light on a different path, a different approach to the subject. In the 1960s and 1970s, Douglas McGregor and James MacGregor Burns launched important assaults on the notion of leadership being an individual characteristic. Further, McGregor argued that it arose from the relationship between variables interacting within the organization. Burns suggested that it was a structure within the organization that impelled it to action. A contemporary of Burns, John Adair, provided a practical description of how leadership operated in meaningful ways at various levels throughout the organization. He also stressed its role in impelling individuals to engage in organizationally meaningful action.

In the 1980s, Kenneth Blanchard offered organizations a flexible and realistic description of a range of basic leadership systems, all of which were perfectly legitimate for application within the same organization, according to the particular circumstances in which any such organization might find itself at any given time. Further, he reversed the traditional view of the relationship between the leader and the employee, arguing that it was the role of the former to serve the latter, rather than the reverse. In so doing, he firmly re-planted the purpose of the leader's position in the service of the organization. For the most part, his work was rejected by academic critics, and was not widely embraced by the modern leadership movement. However, it was enthusiastically welcomed by practitioners in the organizational community. His books sold by the millions, indicating a strong interest in his unique view of how leadership operates in organizations.

Much of import has also been developed about the value of emotional intelligence, and of a comprehensive view of organizational culture. However, perhaps the most insightful inroad toward a proper understanding of leadership in organizations was made by one its earliest modern students. In the first decades of the 20th century, Mary Parker Follett wrote that people had a natural instinct to organize themselves in groups, and that they had natural instincts to manage and direct those groups, as well. More than that, she argued that these groups developed internal dynamics that gave rise to a sort of group dialectic, the product of which was the self-development of goals and the self-management of the group in the pursuit of them. She still accorded certain of the leadership functions, particularly foresight and organizational vision, exclusively to the individual leader at the top. Nevertheless, Follett came to make a vital distinction between authority, which she defined as residing at the top of the organization, and leadership, which she identified as arising naturally from within it. This was a major break-through, pointing the way clearly toward a proper approach for understanding how leadership actually operates in organizations.

Unfortunately, the clear and lucid calls of leadership thinkers, such as Follett and the others mentioned in this section, were lost in the din of the static thrown up by the misinterpretation of the large events transpiring around them. These misinterpretations ultimately gave birth, in the late 20th century, to the modern leadership industry, and culminated in the popping of the leadership bubble, the effects of which we are still observing and struggling with, today.

Full Forward Step

The traditional view of leadership is that it is provided from above to a more or less passive, albeit possibly enthusiastic and receptive, organization. In contrast, the view of organizational leadership as propounded in this book is that it is inherent in the very nature of the organization. It arises from the peculiar rela-tionships that form among people joined together in a collaborative effort. As such, it takes on an identity of its own, existing in these relationships, rather than merely in the individuals who enter into them. Thus, it both influences, and is influenced by, those individuals. It communicates their organizational impres-sions and needs throughout the organization.

From this basis emerges group cohesion. In addition to communication, there is an impulse inherent in the relationship that binds the organization's members to the collaborative effort and to each other. Group cohesion does not arise merely out of a spontaneous spirit of mutual affection or good will. It is a propul-sive force given motion by purpose, and by a joint effort to accomplish it. Com-bined with the natural group identity, and in the medium of collective communication that preceded it, group cohesion begins to produce organiza-tional leadership. This reinforces the existence of a collective identity existing independently of the organization's members. However, this identity is perceived and expressed through those members.

While organizational leadership has a strong bias toward being a positive influ-ence in the organization, it is not so necessarily. It can be hijacked by discontent or simply by bad actors. It can be distorted or corrupted through neglect, and it can become almost an unwitting counterbalance to management, somewhat to the bafflement of both sides. It is often confused for followership, which hobbles its effectiveness. On the other hand, it can be cultivated through proper attention to the organization's group cohesion, and managed effectively for the benefit of the organization and, ultimately, all of its members.

BENEFITS

Organizational leadership is a characteristic inevitably inherent in the organization. As long as there is an organization, organizational leadership is there, for the having or the asking. It is either active and can be harnessed, or it is a potential that can be developed and cultivated. Organizational leadership is robust, or it is latent, to the extent that group cohesion exists and is in harmony with the organization's goals. There certainly are organizations where group cohesion is a feeble, or even a seemingly non-existent, force. In such organizations, organizational leadership has likely been cut off at the knees by the attempts of traditional leaders, jealous of their prerogatives or willfully heedless of the contributions of others, to repress or straightjacket group cohesion. Fortunately, it is an enduringly vital and natural element that is always ready to respond to intelligent management. The benefits of such management are considerable. They are both direct and indirect in nature, and they are both additive and exponential in their contribution to the organization's efforts. Moreover, they can be enjoyed almost immediately upon recognition of organizational leadership's existence and true nature, together with conscientious efforts to properly manage it.

Managers

Management begins by accepting its subservient role as managers of the organization's assets, including its organizational leadership, rather than assuming an unsustainably supreme role as its leader, whose leadership the organization serves merely to express. Management acknowledges that the organization is a dynamic, constructive entity eager to contribute positively to organizational goals, not a generally passive weight requiring constant effort to inspire and manipulate into action.

On realizing that organizational leadership is a powerful asset waiting to be constructively engaged in the organization's efforts, management applies to it traditional managerial attention. It both consumes and sustains its organizational leadership. It uses that leadership by marshaling and deploying it as discussed in

Chapter 7. Management also sustains it by paying judicious and consistent attention to the organization's group cohesion.

Such efforts, rather than merely a necessary expenditure to generate sporadic
or reluctant activity from naturally passive or recalcitrant employees, create self-
generating and tangible benefits for managers. To begin with, management of
organizational leadership relieves managers of many of the overarching expectations that have heretofore been placed on them. These pressures for the possession of seemingly infallible vision and foresight, for the personal expression of the
leadership functions, and for a wizard-like mastery over events and the behavior
of the organization, have proven time after time to be fundamentally unbearable.
It is incumbent upon all of us to pay attention to the man behind the curtain.
After all, our own unrealistic expectations of him played a large part in driving
him there. The basic lack of integrity in the assumption by any single individual
of such a false mantle of charismatic leadership erodes the cohesive force of the
fiduciary obligations that properly bind together an organization, its executives,
its owners, and the larger community. In turn, this has led, or contributed substantially, to many of the scandals, failures, and simple disappointments that still
beset organizational life.

To relieve management of such burdens is no small feat, and it confers no
small measure of advantage and benefit on all concerned. Now, management can
settle more comfortably into its proper role in the service of the organization,
alongside its other employees. Rather than attempt to personally express all of the
organization's leadership, it can marshal, deploy, and manage leadership on
behalf of the organization that will prove far more comprehensive of the organization's opportunities and needs, and far more effective in addressing them.
Finally, management can turn more of its attention to matters properly in its
exclusive purview, and which have, perhaps to the ultimate adversity of all, suffered from neglect.

Employees

As many observers have noted, the modern economy is rapidly shifting to a
knowledge basis. Increasingly, the measurement of employees' contributions is
moving away from what physical actions they perform, or how they manipulate
equipment or inputs as these pass through the production process. Rather, it is
the knowledge and skills that they bring to the enterprise that is valued and com-
pensated. Machines or processes are able to accomplish, today, what human labor
was relied on for, previously. As competition and the accumulation and process-

ing of information become more immediate influences on organizational activity, individual abilities to comprehend and address these issues are of mounting importance.

Consequently, the concept of the knowledge worker has gained currency. This refers to an employee who brings uniquely individual creative contributions to the enterprise. These abilities are a product of personal education and training, and of their application, in creative ways, to the situation at hand. Management thinkers have concluded that this has required management to adapt by viewing employees as a dynamic resource to be led, rather than as an essentially passive, but unavoidable, organizational feature to be controlled.

Further, as Peter Drucker has notably observed, the modern knowledge worker is developing what might properly be viewed as the executive mindset. That is, he looks for ways to contribute, and measures his own value by his success in doing so. Thus, it may be concluded that management's role in such circumstances is to find outlets for that impulse to contribute. After all, even if the impulse is not consciously there, it is inherent in the character of knowledge work and can be easily drawn out.

It is more accurate, though, to say that the modern knowledge worker, knowingly or otherwise possessed of a fundamentally executive mindset, is a full participant in the endeavors of the organization. Such an employee has not merely hired on—he has bought in (figuratively speaking). He has cohered. He is now as meaningfully involved in the ultimate struggle for success of the organization as is management. Many have argued that the modern phenomenon of job mobility—of the tendency to view one's self as one's own employer, contracting out to this or that firm as deemed appropriate—is corrosive of employee loyalty or group cohesion. However, managerial mobility is no less a reality, nor less a potentially corrosive force on the organizational integrity of a firm. It is when that independent spirit willingly harnesses itself to a particular enterprise that group cohesion rallies and organizational leadership thrives. In addition, it is effective management, unleashing the leadership inherent in the modern organization, which enables this. Leadership imposed on such employees is increasingly recognized as fundamentally patronizing and manipulative, and dismissive of their real abilities to contribute. Management of those capabilities, and of their expression through organizational leadership, is what is called for.

Boards

The truth is that, while the great preponderance of criticism over organizational failures has fallen on the heads of their senior executives, it belongs, more properly, to their boards of directors. After all, management can only be expected to participate enthusiastically in the natural struggle for power and maneuver room that is a major and inescapable feature of any collective enterprise. What's more, they can be expected to participate with degrees of skill and staying power that usually cannot be met by their boards. For one thing, they are full-time players, unlike their boards. Further, they tend to have closer and greater knowledge about the organization, and the consequent ability to manipulate that knowledge to their advantage in the course of their struggle for power with the board. Certainly, this should be partially countered by the fact that many board members are prominent and successful professional executives from other organizations, fully aware of these abilities and tendencies of management. However, this very fact sometimes operates as a subtle, but powerful, co-opting force, restraining the assertive behavior of these outside board members.

That, however, is an explanation and not an excuse. There is no avoiding the fact that all of these directors are legitimately presumed to have been selected, through one means or another, by owners, or other legal creators of the organization, to represent their interests—not those of management. As simple and readily agreeable a concept as this is, it is widely neglected. Boards take on an advisory role. Fearful of overstepping their bounds, and intruding into the management of the organization, they are careful to keep their distance. They tell themselves that their real role is to guide, advise, facilitate, use their contacts to the benefit of the organization, and, perhaps, to act as a brake of final resort should things go too far astray. Unfortunately, they do not tend to step into that latter function until things have already gone too far astray. Regarding their other typical activities, while on the surface there doesn't seem to be anything wrong with supporting management's efforts, where appropriate, and helping to develop the skills of individual managers, that simply is not the board's real role. Its actual role is to represent the interests of owners. This is done by hiring managers, setting policy for them, and then proactively ensuring that they are acting within the bounds of that policy.

A major factor behind the confusion regarding these issues among boards, today, is the high volume of static surrounding the propaganda of charismatic individual leadership produced by the modern leadership movement. According to this, leaders have capabilities, the expression of which must be facilitated and supported so that the organization can most effectively act on them. Often, these abilities are beyond the ken of those who do not naturally possess them, or who have not yet developed them, depending on which wing of the movement is consulted. The non-comprehension of the visionary musings of charismatic leaders by board members is thus taken as validation of the veracity of that individual leadership, rather than as a signal that some common sense needs to be proactively applied to the developing situation. It is to be remembered, as well, that many of the board members are the singular charismatic leaders of other organizations. They know how to play the leadership game.

Nevertheless, increasingly, through legislation or litigation, boards are going to have their feet held to the fire. They have growing incentives to examine their proper duties and responsibilities, and to rationalize their own organization and activities around them. An important way for them to redress the balance of power between them and management is for them to return the managers they have hired to their proper roles. The acquiescence to the functioning of individual leadership in their senior executives carries with it a concomitant obligation to acquiesce to the demands of that leadership. To do otherwise is inherently contradictory, and is subject to criticism as such. However, adoption of the view of organizational leadership propounded in this book enables boards to regain control over both the management and the leadership of the organization. This is done, not by assuming either, but by supervising both. Thus, the board can promote the rationalization of the management of the organizational leadership of their organizations by establishing it as policy and overseeing its implementation. Moreover, they can legitimately use the expression of that organizational leadership, themselves, to help them do that.

Organizations

Organizations are powerful tools for the accomplishment of large enterprises. They are also the settings where not only the ability to support one's self and one's family is derived, but where important measures of psychic well being are generated. This takes the form of individual achievement and contribution, of course, but also of these things in the context of social interaction and collaboration. Further, the role played by organizational efforts in the context of the larger community and society is an influential factor in the capability for healthy and rewarding adaptation, adjustment, and growth of individuals, and their ability to contribute to their own well being and that of others. Organizations are important institutions of the larger culture. Their integrity is a thing of value; it is worth making the effort to understand them, and to give them strength and vitality.

However, they are also complex congeries of a wide range of individually fragile, and sometimes unrelated—sometimes even contradictory—forces and factors. They are difficult to get right and to manage. In such situations, events periodically conspire to cause one or more of their constituent elements to start to unravel. Like a spider web, the strength of which lies in the totality of its design and unity of construction, rather than in merely the additive force of its component strands, an organization can lose its inherent integrity at many points, leading to loss of efficiency, and even to potentially destructive imbalances.

It is certainly important for students of organizations to continually work to identify the multitude of influences, elements, and factors that make up and operate in groups. However, that is not enough. They ought to study, as well, the integrity of design and dynamic interaction that enables organizations to maintain, at the same time, elasticity, and a purposeful and recognizable structure. It is the well understood and managed combination of these that enable executives to achieve and maintain organizational equilibrium.

Identifying all of these is an incredibly complex task and, while it ought to be pursued, it is likely to elude completion for some time. It is probably too much, as well, to expect any of an organization's component parts, even professional management, to identify and dynamically coordinate all of these things. But the release within an organization of its own inherent leadership can go a long way toward helping it to maintain both its equilibrium, and its ability to adapt to changing circumstances as it pursues its aim. It will help to maintain, in other words, its organizational integrity. This is not meant to suggest that it can magically monitor and preserve the integrity of each one of all the multitudes of components of the organization. But by addressing itself to the principle load-bearing structures, in particular the employees, management, and ownership, and to the design of their interaction, it can help to both monitor and preserve their individual and collective integrity as an organization. This is likely not only to benefit it as a closed system, but as an open one in intimate contact with its surroundings.

Of more immediate concern, perhaps, is the issue of the integrity of the operations of the organization. The intelligently managed self-expression of organizational leadership within it will make them more focused, more informed in design and efficient in application, and more adaptive and productively tuned to the ultimate purpose of the organization. Whether witnessed in the dramatic behavior of individual soldiers in a military unit in combat, or in the incremental contributions of production floor employees to a policy of continuous improvement, organizational leadership can directly and powerfully benefit the entire organization, to the extent to which it is properly understood and managed.

IMPLEMENTATION AND THE BOARD

As mentioned previously, however obviously laudable—or even stipulated to as superior—they may be, actions and policies tend to be more reliably pursued when they are backed by practical, as well as moral, authority. Therefore, the reliable and consistent application of the concept of management of organizational leadership begins not with managers, but with boards of directors. As the representatives of owners, they have the necessary standing to cause policies to be implemented by management. They are also at sufficient distance from the daily operations of the company and machinations of its executives to apply balanced perspective to the direction and supervision of their policies.

Boards cannot properly manage their organizations. Their role, rather, is to direct that management. They can set policy and proactively direct management's compliance with it. The ultimate result of such board behavior, far from restraining management's robustness and reducing it to a tame, demoralized force in the company, should be to firmly set it on its authorized path, and arm it with the ability to decisively and energetically follow it. The idea that strong boards and strong management cannot coexist is not necessarily true. If they understand and properly manage their respective roles and contributions, they can each benefit and draw additional strength for themselves from that displayed by the other. Management that understands its proper relationship to the organization and the board is ready, in turn, to get its marching orders from the board. Further, it is ready to operate decisively based on those orders, fully confident that it is doing so within the parameters of its remit. There is a meeting of minds, which releases energy from occupying itself in conflict and the struggle for power, and allows it to direct itself to the productive service of the enterprise.

The adoption by boards of the concept of organizational leadership will help them to reassess and reestablish the basis of their relationships with management. By clarifying the roles of all the key players of the organization, the concept will allow boards to encourage and enable all of those players to more effectively and productively combine their efforts to accomplish its goals. Yet, however fine that all sounds, the actual doing of it must consist in practical and concrete actions by the board. These begin with selection of the senior executive.

The Senior Executive

In an essay entitled "Self Reliance," Ralph Waldo Emerson said, "an institution is the lengthened shadow of one man." This was written to show that the great structures of society and movements of history could be traced back to the actions of individual men. It was meant to discourage conformity, and encourage the daring of great enterprises. In the preface, I criticized this sentiment as promoting unwarranted daring in the persons of those at the head of today's great organizations.

However, it can also, if taken in a slightly different context, hint at an important truth, one that boards would do well to consider. This is that organizations do tend to reflect the personalities of their bosses. That is not to say that they mimic it, but that they adapt themselves to it. If the boss is abrasive, the organization may become hesitant and cowed. If he is a micromanaging perfectionist, it may become bureaucratic and inwardly focused. If he is arrogant and swaggering, it may become overflowing with loose cannons all going off with great, roaring enthusiasm, but questionable accuracy.

On the other hand, if he is focused on doing his duty, contributing, himself, and facilitating the contributions of others, it is likely to form up and work hard along with him. This is the sort of senior executive that boards should look for.

It is not appropriate for a board to ask candidates for the senior executive position their vision for the future of the company. The candidates ought not to be treated as though they are auditioning for a role in a play, but are also being asked to explain how they will write it. They should be told what that vision is, and asked how they intend to realize it. The board should listen attentively for the candidates' views on management, and even more attentively—and skeptically—to any views they might volunteer about leadership.

Many commentators have made various observations about the combinations of virtues to be sought in senior executives, and how missing ones can affect the value of the others. Among the most telling is General von Manstein's suggestion that the officer who is smart and lazy makes the best commander; a commander who knows how to prioritize, who will naturally focus on the most important issues, and who will ignore the others as wastes of his, and his organization's, time. We might not appreciate that laziness appears to be standing in for the courage of one's convictions, but we should appreciate the persistence it represents to preserve organizational energy for focused application on the issues of true import for it. After all, then, these are a most useful pair of attributes to keep an eye out for.

Moreover, they point to another attribute of importance. That is the presence of integrity. This term is commonly taken to mean honesty and truthfulness. The core meaning, however, is more comprehensive. It refers to a characteristic completeness, or wholeness, about something. It suggests that the thing referred to is actually what it represents itself to be. Anyone who ascribes to himself the charismatic qualities of leadership isn't likely to possess integrity in its fullest sense, and neither, ultimately, will any organization he heads. However, one who does possess integrity in this broader sense will insist on its possession by all—by his board, his management staff, and his organization. He will want them all to be what they represent themselves to be. He will insist upon being held accountable, and will hold others accountable, as well. In other words, he will not view integrity as an exclusively personal quality, but one that must exist throughout the organization. The lack of it, anywhere, will compromise the ability of everyone, everywhere, to exhibit it.

This is the type of senior executive a board should seek. He will recognize and work to fulfill his role in the organization. Moreover, he will deploy all assets available to him to do so, including those inherent in the organization itself—such as the phenomenon of organizational leadership.

CONCLUSION

The idea that organizations possess the quality of self-management, if not self-leadership, has been around since Mary Follett began writing about it in the early 20th century. Since then, other observers have noted the extra-individual quality of leadership in an organizational setting—its character of somehow existing, and operating independently of, the organization's individual members. Some have ascribed it to relationships between levels of control or power in the group. Others have accorded it limited measures of the qualities of leadership, reserving the most important expressions of that to the leader at the top.

With this book, however, I have hoped to encourage boards and managers to see leadership as neither some ineffable entity independent of the organization, nor as a set of individual characteristics used to bring an organization to life, but rather as a perfectly comprehensible phenomenon that arises normally and inevitably from the organization itself. It is always there. It may be bruised when individual leaders attempt to hijack it to their own self-aggrandizement, or are themselves hoodwinked into thinking that that is what they are expected—and thus compelled—to do. However, it will recover under the influence of intelligent management, which leverages organizational leadership's value as a powerful asset always available to the organization.

It is my hope that I will have convinced enough readers to begin a debate on this topic that redirects the attention of professional students and practitioners of management back to the line of thinking begun by Mary Follett so long ago. I hope that boards, informed with the insights humbly proffered in this book, will begin the search for, and impel the development of, more organizationally attuned and effective senior executives—executives who can be guided toward a new and usable understanding of what leadership really is—and how to manage it.

Notes

1. Studies of military leadership generally focus on military organizations serving state or other internationally recognized actors; this discussion refers to such military organizations.

2. The term *soldier* will be used herein to refer generically to the military, due to the ordinary tendency of non-military people to do so, and to avoid burdening the dialogue with pointless precision. Certainly, all of this applies to all military personnel of all Services, as well, whether male or female.

3. Marshall's assertions in the book, regarding the low ratios of fire employed by American servicemen in combat in World War II, immediately generated vigorous debate throughout the military. Additionally, more than thirty years after its initial publication, questions were raised regarding the precision of his methodology, and of the data he reported on that specific claim. Whatever the merits of those concerns, they neither address nor obviate the astuteness and veracity of the insights of the unusually well-positioned, experienced, perceptive, and articulate observer of the behavior of men under fire in combat units that Marshall clearly was. It is these insights that are employed in the present work.

4. Marshall spent the years between the World Wars as a civilian journalist, and was well situated to note the similarities and differences between military and civilian organizations. On a number of occasions in *Men Against Fire*, he comments on the parallels between the two in matters—not of leadership—but of human behavior and initiative as displayed in the context of organizations.

5. The Silver Star is the third highest US military award for heroism in combat.

6. US commanding officers were particularly vulnerable to enemy fire during combat, both because the enemy considered them to be valuable targets, and because their command duties prevented them from paying sufficient attention to their own safety. Accordingly, during combat engagements, the unit

driver, who was not otherwise assigned a combat role in a line unit, was customarily seconded as the commanding officer's bodyguard. This arrangement gave the commanding officer some needed protection, freeing him to focus on his command duties with less distraction, and also provided an important and valued role for the driver during combat.

7. Colonel Williams always struck us as an officer of indestructible calm and steadiness of purpose. He was not given to swaggering bravado or heroism, but rather to a quiet but unswerving determination to advance his entire unit toward mission accomplishment. That we discovered him also to be one of the famous "Gunfighters" is yet another lesson that, while heroes may be born of individual characteristics, or of circumstances, leadership of this caliber is born of these combined with extraordinary group cohesion. Just as his men would have done anything for their captain, they knew he would have done anything for them. Captain Williams was himself a product of the group cohesion that he helped cultivate to an intense degree in his unit. This group cohesion generated an insuperable collective will and force in his unit, expressed in a combined aggressive desire to advance, and in individual expressions of courage, sacrifice, and heroism throughout, including, notably, from Captain Williams himself. But where gunfighters were called for, they were all gunfighters.

8. Captain Williams proved himself profoundly ready to serve his country, his mission, and his Marines. He was later awarded a second Silver Star, a Purple Heart for injuries suffered while earning that second award, and a Bronze Star, also for his heroism displayed in combat. Further, throughout a distinguished career, Colonel Williams instinctively demonstrated a rare appreciation of organizational leadership, which he incisively used to develop and implement farsighted initiatives, which remain enduringly positive and influential forces in the Marine Corps.

9. This is a military saying arising from the special legal and moral nature of commissioned service which, while unique, is nevertheless comparable to the general fiduciary responsibilities assumed by senior executives in non-military organizations. An irony, which turns this saying on its head, is that juniors are all too often delegated responsibility for a task without being delegated the authority necessary to accomplish it.

10. In this instance, the term *responsibility* is used in a broad sense, reflecting shared commitment arising from strong group cohesion, rather than the technical sense of legal or fiduciary responsibility, discussed in the previous chapter.

11. Ironically, these administrative structures in civilian organizations are often strikingly more autocratic and uncommunicative than the executives in these same organizations assume to be the case in the military.

12. Verifiable information permitting the full citation of this article in future editions of this book may be e-mailed to feedback@managingleadership.com

13. Direct responsibility (or authority) is derived from ownership and is complete. It is contrasted here with derived responsibility (or authority), which is awarded to hired management, and is contractually defined and delimited.

14. Additional critiques are welcomed for consideration for inclusion in future editions of this book. Please e-mail them to critiques@ managingleadership.com

15. One might point out that, while I am arguing here that pre-modern examples of leadership, such as those from Imperial Rome, are not legitimate for use in today's modern world of collaborative, corporate enterprises, I have nevertheless quoted an Imperial Roman Emperor, Marcus Aurelius, at the beginning of Chapter 5. That, of course, is true. But then, he is not known for his leadership, in the premodern sense of the word. He is renowned precisely for his insights, gathered in the *Meditations of Marcus Aurelius*, which explain how the individual leader should view himself as under obligation to his ties to the led, rather than the reverse.

Suggestions for Further Reading

The selection of books below is principally by authors discussed in Chapter 3. Henri Fayol, who was not referred to in this book, has been added to this list. He is a contemporary of Mary Parker Follett, although he worked and wrote in France. He was not particularly well acknowledged there, but became quite influential after his work was published in the United States in the 1950s. He has been called the father of the school of administrative management, and has insightful observations on the topic of command authority. I have also included, here, two works by Kurt Lewin, who was referred to in Chapter 6 for his studies of leadership styles and his force field theory. Finally, Peter Drucker, referred to in Chapters 7 and 9, is also included, here. He is widely recognized as the first, and perhaps foremost, professional student of management.

Adair, John (1984). *Action-centered leadership*. Maidenhead: McGraw-Hill.

Blanchard, Kenneth H. (1985). *Leadership and the one minute manager*. New York: Morrow.

Blanchard, Kenneth H., Carew, Donald & Parisi-Carew, Eunice (2000). *The one minute manager builds high performing teams*. New York: Wm. Morrow and Co.

Burns, James M. (1978). *Leadership*. New York: Harper & Row.

Drucker, Peter F. (1967). *The Effective Executive*. New York: Harper & Row.

Fayol, Henri (1984). *General and industrial management*. (Rev. ed.). New York: Institute of Electrical and Electronics Engineers.

Follett, Mary P. (1973). *Dynamic administration; the collected papers of Mary Parker Follett*. (Elliot M. Fox and L. Urwick, Eds.). London: Pitman.

Follett, Mary P. (1987). *Freedom & co-ordination: lectures in business organization*. New York: Garland Pub.

Graham, Pauline (Ed.). (1995). *Mary Parker Follett—prophet of management: a celebration of writings from the 1920s.* Boston, Mass: Harvard Business School Press.

Lewin, Kurt (1975). *Field theory in social science; selected theoretical papers.* (Dorwin Cartwright, Ed.). Westport, Conn: Greenwood Press.

Lewin, Kurt (1997). *Resolving social conflicts; &,Field theory in social science.* Washington, DC: American Psychological Association.

Marshall, S. L. A. (2000). *Men against fire: the problem of battlefield command.* Norman, Oklahoma: University of Oklahoma Press

Maslow, Abraham H. (1993). *The farther reaches of human nature.* New York: Arkana.

Maslow, Abraham H. [with new material by Ruth Cox and Robert Frager] (1987). *Motivation and personality.* New York: Harper and Row.

McGregor, Douglas (1960). *The human side of enterprise.* New York: McGraw-Hill.

About the Author

Jim Stroup is a management consultant specializing in organizational leadership. Born and raised in Detroit, Michigan, Jim began his working career with stints in a diner, several gas stations, a tool and die shop, and in an advertising agency mail room. During this period, his academic career went into a long hiatus after two years studying philosophy and history. After a few years, he moved to North Dakota to take a job as a common laborer on a construction site.

Later, Jim enlisted in the U.S. Marine Corps, and served as an Infantry Marine in the United States and Japan, as well as on deployments to the Mediterranean and the Western Pacific. After several years, and promotion to the rank of sergeant, Jim was selected for a commissioning program. As an Infantry Officer, he continued to serve as a commander and staff officer in the operating forces in Hawaii, with further deployments to the Western Pacific and Indian Oceans. Upon assignment to a major training command on the West Coast, he was instrumental in the expansion and development of three major specialty certification and professional development programs. Later, Jim served in the first Gulf War, in 1990 and 1991. During his spare time in this period, Jim also completed his bachelor's degree, magna cum laude, in international relations, and a master's degree with a dual concentration in business and management.

Jim subsequently entered the Marine Corps Foreign Area Officer program, and went to the Defense Language Institute in Monterey, California, where he learned Arabic. Next, he and his family moved to Cairo, Egypt, where they lived for a year while Jim traveled throughout the Middle East, honing his skills as a military expert for the area. During this time, he also managed to obtain certification as a foreign area officer for Europe, with a specialty for Turkey. After serving a further tour as the operations advisor for the Kuwait Ground Forces, Jim retired and turned to work in the civilian world, during which period he also found time to complete a doctorate in business administration.

During and since his military career, Jim has had the opportunity to work with, observe, and advise numerous military and civilian organizations, from many countries and cultures, on four continents. He has developed substantial expertise in organizational leadership, and he consults widely and writes on this subject, as well as other related organizational and management topics.

Jim is married and lives in Istanbul, Turkey. While still in the United States, his wife, Emel, obtained her doctorate in clinical psychology. She is also a certified cognitive therapist, and she practices and teaches in Istanbul. Jim and Emel have one son, Tarik, who is a graduate of the visual arts program at the University of California, San Diego, and who lives and works in his field in Southern California.

Index

Numerics

3M 112

A

Ability xiii, xiv, xvi, 13, 18, 20, 21, 22, 32, 33, 42, 49, 51, 53, 65, 69, 70, 76, 78, 80, 86, 87, 90, 96, 97, 107, 109, 115, 117, 123, 125, 132, 133, 134, 135, 137

Academic 5, 6, 11, 30, 127, 145

Accountability 7, 85, 86, 124

Achievement 28, 74, 77, 110, 133

Action 11, 24, 28, 29, 30, 33, 44, 47, 48, 49, 51, 55, 56, 61, 66, 67, 68, 73, 74, 77, 91, 94, 95, 96, 97, 98, 120, 127, 129, 143

Action-Centered Leadership 11, 24, 30, 143

Adair, John 11, 24, 30, 127, 143

Adaptation 57, 94, 133

Additive 129, 134

Adjustment 133

Administration 7, 57, 58, 117, 143, 145

Advance 13, 26, 34, 47, 50, 51, 55, 56, 68, 76, 89, 91, 140

Advanced Forward Incrementors 13

Advantage 3, 30, 62, 74, 80, 91, 120, 130, 132

Advice 33, 83, 84, 98, 114, 115

Affirmation 97

Agent of Change 13

Aggressive 71, 140

Aim xiv, 76, 89, 95, 134

Alexander the Great 109, 110

Analysis 16, 41, 45, 65, 70, 83, 92

Anxiety 78

Apathy 73, 80

Assessment 65, 87, 112

Asset xiii, xv, xviii, 15, 36, 67, 78, 81, 91, 93, 95, 115, 117, 129, 138

Assistance 83, 84, 111

Assumptions xvi, 68, 124

Attention xvi, 9, 10, 15, 20, 26, 29, 30, 32, 36, 45, 47, 63, 67, 72, 74, 75, 85, 86, 97, 99, 110, 116, 117, 121, 129, 130, 138, 139

Attribute 12, 65, 72, 137

Attribution Theory 12

Authority xiii, xviii, 9, 10, 18, 19, 22, 34, 43, 56, 57, 58, 59, 60, 61, 62, 64, 84, 86, 92, 94, 96, 98, 113, 114, 115, 119, 120, 123, 128, 135, 140, 141, 143

Authority Model 10

Autocratic 71, 72, 73, 76, 80, 84, 92, 141

B

Battle 44, 45, 47, 49, 66, 103

Battlefield 44, 47, 48, 50, 144

Behavior xvi, 11, 12, 23, 34, 42, 43, 44, 45, 46, 47, 48, 49, 51, 54, 60, 65, 71, 79, 106, 107, 108, 117, 118, 130, 132, 134, 135, 139

Belbin, R. Meredith 24

Benefit 34, 48, 50, 54, 68, 80, 89, 91, 92, 98, 111, 112, 116, 118, 120, 121, 129, 130, 132, 134, 135

Bias 74, 95, 128

Blanchard, Kenneth 31, 32, 127, 143

Board xviii, 14, 17, 21, 22, 57, 58, 59, 60, 86, 88, 95, 96, 112, 119, 132, 133, 135, 136, 137

Boldness 44

0-595-31551-8